Praise for
THE GIFT OF CONFESSION:
POSITIVE APPROACH TO THE SACRAMENT OF RECONCILIATION

"Given the fall off in recent years it is refreshing to find a book that urges people to take up again the practice of confessing their sins. Readers will be moved and convinced by the real spiritual benefits of Confession. These benefits go beyond the forgiveness of sins to the wider and perhaps, today, the more fundamental matter of reorienting ones life towards Christ. This is a book about God's unfailing mercy."
Most Rev B J Hickey, Archbishop of Perth

"Father Michael de Stoop is to be congratulated for producing an easy to read book by young and old, by the learned and the less educated. In a word the book is 'Catholic', i.e. embracing everyone who can read. As he states in the Conclusion: "the Sacrament of Reconciliation is a gift, not a burden." That the wide practice of Confession in times prior to the Ecumenical Council of Vatican II (1962-1965) can be restored will be disputed only by the pessimists."
Most Rev Luc Matthys, Bishop of Armidale

"We often hear that the Sacrament of reconciliation is in crisis today. But every crisis is a 'growing pain.' Indeed, many people today are discovering that this wonderful sacrament does far more than alleviate guilt; it brings the penitent into the loving embrace of the Father. I pray that this gem of a book brings more and more people to this realisation."
Rev Fr Michael Kennedy, PP, STL, Wagga Wagga Diocese

"Father Michael de Stoop has addressed the problem of the Sacrament of Reconciliation being regarded as a mechanical procedure rather than a genuine encounter with God's mercy. I recommend his book, "The Gift of Confession" is an ideal aide for young people who wish to participate in the World Youth Day experience. Others will discover the hidden riches of this great gift of Jesus Christ to those who wish to participate to the full in the Paschal Mystery."
Most Rev Peter J Connors, Bishop of Ballarat

"This book could be entitled Confession in a Nutshell or Confession for Dummies. It contains all the basic information about sin and grace which holy nuns once imparted to children. However, it is accessible to all age groups and will be of value for those who missed out on this kind of intellectual content in their sacramental programs when they were children.

The work is up to date with references to Scripture and to the Catechism of the Catholic Church. It is a presentation of the Church's official teaching as it stands in the Pontificate of Benedict XVI but with the addition of Fr de Stoop's personal reflections on the value of the sacrament based on his own pastoral experience."

Dr Tracey Rowland, Dean - John Paul II Institute, Melbourne

The Gift of Confession:

A Positive Approach to the Sacrament of Reconciliation

25 Benefits for you

GRACEWING

First published in Australia by Connor Court Publishing Pty Ltd

This edition published in England 2007

Gracewing
2 Southern Avenue, Leominster
Herefordshire, HR6 0QF

Nihil Obstat: Rev Peter Joseph, STD

Imprimatur: George Cardinal Pell, Archbishop of Sydney
30 April 2007, Feast of Saint Pope Pius V

Acknowledgement of Standard Texts:

Catechism of the Catholic Church (Second Edition), Homebush, Sydney: St Paul's Publications, 1994.

Quotations from the Scriptures are from the *Revised Standard Version Catholic Edition (RSVCE)*, Princeton, NJ: Scepter © 1966, or when stated from the *Jerusalem Bible (JB)* London: Geoffrey Chapman, 1971, © 1968 by Darton Longman and Todd Ltd and Doubleday & Co., Inc

Front cover and hand illustrations: Richard de Stoop www.richarddestoop.com

ISBN 978 0 85244 514 3

Printed in England

Contents

Dedicated to my parents, Paul and Christine,
in appreciation of their love for me,
for they have given me a window
through which I first discovered
divine mercy.

THE GIFT OF CONFESSION

Foreword by George Cardinal Pell

Father Michael de Stoop has written another good book, this time on "The Gift of Confession: A Positive Approach to the Sacrament of Reconciliation," listing 25 benefits. He knows what he is writing about and draws wisely on his priestly experience. I believe that this short work will help people of all age groups, but especially young Catholic leaders.

For more than a decade now the Spirit has been moving in a particular way among some young Australian adults, workers, university graduates, even school leavers, who have volunteered for a year, and often longer to give witness to Christ and the Church among their peers in parishes, schools and groups.

Father Michael has been involved in the care and formation of the Sydney Archdiocese Catholic Youth Service team and more recently with an Australian and New Zealand group of young adults following a three month intensive formation course for World Youth Day in 2008. He knows these young leaders and the many different types of young Australians with whom they work. He knows that most young adult Catholics, especially with some explanation and encouragement, are pleased to go "to confession."

I am not sure that the author is right to claim that "a declining number of Catholics" are participating in this sacrament. There is little doubt that numbers are at rock bottom in many places, but I suspect the tide is turning.

The willingness of members of Generation Y to talk honestly about their problems and hurts is a surprise to their elders, and there is some evidence that this openness extends beyond young Catholics. I heard of a recent group of young Australian soldiers on their way to a war zone. Perhaps a third of them were Catholics, but about two thirds went to the Catholic priest chaplain to "confess." The collapse of inter-denominational religious prejudice has produced some surprising fruits!

The Catholic Church has survived over the centuries despite many mistakes and one of the worst mistakes of the last forty years was to persuade believers, young and old, that personal confession of serious sins was a mistake and unnecessary. This was "Catholic lite" at its most ineffectual, another failure to understand fallen human nature and popular psychology.

We all need forgiveness as we need to deal with our guilt; some more than others, either because of their personality or because of their "track record" and the Church has given us this wonderful Sacrament, this healing ritual which Father Michael explains so well.

I pray, and anticipate, that this book will touch the hearts and enlighten the minds of many saints and sinners, teachers and witnesses.

✠ George Cardinal Pell,
Archbishop of Sydney

Introduction

Even before I became a priest I always found Confession a positive experience. Now as a priest I try to make this sacrament meaningful for others. Even though many priests are working hard to make God's mercy accessible we are still seeing a declining number of Catholics availing themselves of this sacrament.

Given that this is the case, I think there is every reason to believe that there are a growing number of people who are unaware of the theology that helps us to understand and appreciate this sacrament. This begs the question, how can the Church encourage people to have a renewed interest and appreciation for this sacrament if they do not know why we need it? Perhaps this question can be best answered in light of a prevailing attitude we are most familiar with: our consumer society has conditioned us to ask ourselves such things as, "What do I get out of it? What is in it for me?" Surely in this context the best way of promoting Confession is to educate people about the many *benefits* we receive from it. It is to that end that I have set myself the task of writing this book.

Focusing upon what we receive from this sacrament is relevant in these times because many people only think of it in terms of its power to forgive our sins. However, if you have at least read the contents page at this point you will be prepared to see that Confession gives us much more than it takes away! Taking "negative" things (sin) away is one thing for which this sacrament is well known, but how many people think of the Sacrament of Reconciliation in terms of the "positive" things it provides for us? Some of the benefits enumerated in this book share a number of things in common. Nevertheless, having specified them according to these twenty-five categories may prove to be helpful because they are things that we can relate to and appreciate.

In presenting these benefits I have cited the Church's teachings, relevant Scripture passages, and the insights of some of the saints, together with my own theological reflections. Such content is given that the reader may be convinced that there are good reasons that this sacrament does indeed provide us with many profound benefits. Due to his ability to provide a profound and deep understanding of our Faith, I have also quoted on numerous occasions what Archbishop Fulton Sheen (1895-1979) said on the various things which touch on these topics. Sheen was a famous author and orator who had a tremendous gift of being able to make the truths of Christianity appealing and easy to understand through the use of good analogies, stories and pithy sayings. He was one of the first to use the medium of television to evangelise by presenting live broadcasts entitled, *Life is Worth Living* from 1951 to 1957. This was the most popular program during that time in the United States, drawing as many as thirty million people on a weekly basis. In 2002 Sheen's cause for canonization was officially opened, so he is now referred to as a Servant of God.

Having cited the works of those who make the Mysteries of our Faith easy to understand, this may prove to be a helpful resource for priests, pastoral associates, sacramental coordinators, Catholic school teachers, catechists, etc, in their efforts to educate the growing number of Catholics who are taking for granted how helpful the Sacrament of Reconciliation is in the Christian life. It is my hope that this book may also help the laity, especially those who have strayed from the practice of their faith, as it may encourage them to have a greater vested interest in this sacrament.

I began by stating that a declining number of Catholics are coming to Confession, but I am aware that priests themselves are partly to blame for this. Parishioners often complain that they never hear their parish priests preach about this sacrament. Where this is the case, priests may find these twenty-five chapters useful. For example, taking one chapter at a time and integrating it into their homily wherever appropriate may be one way by which they can promote this sacrament. Looking for opportunities to catechise the faithful about the Sacrament of Reconciliation is something that I personally see as important today due to the widespread loss of the sense of sin. Pope John Paul II said to the

German Bishops, "I am convinced that a rebirth of the moral conscience and of Christian life is strictly and indissolubly bound up with one condition: the revitalization of personal Confession. Give this priority in your pastoral effort." The following words of his have also been of inspiration to me:

> *Pastors who are zealous and creative never lack opportunities for imparting this broad and varied catechesis, taking into account the different degrees of education and religious formation of those to whom they speak. Such opportunities are often given by the biblical readings and the rites of the Mass and the sacraments, as also by the circumstances of their celebration. For the same purpose many initiatives can be taken such as sermons, lectures, discussions, meetings, courses of religious education, etc., as happens in many places.*[1]

It is my hope that this book will inspire priests and those involved in Catholic education to look for new ways to encourage the faithful to have a greater appreciation for the Sacrament of Reconciliation.

[1] *Reconciliation and Penance in the Mission of the Church Today (Reconciliatio et Paenitentia)*, 1984, no. 26.

Chapter One

God's Mercy is Communicated in a Tangible Way

We are not disembodied spirits. Unlike the angels we rely upon our senses of sight, hearing, touch, smell and taste to encounter God. That is why the sacraments are so special as they make visible and tangible the invisible Mystery of God. By communicating God's love for us and revealing His activity in our lives, the sacraments enable us to be deeply touched as we encounter Christ through our own senses.

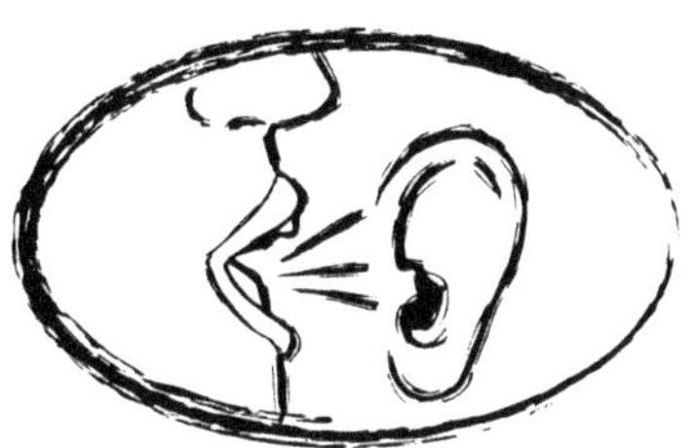

The Sacrament of Reconciliation (otherwise known as the *Sacrament of Penance* or *Confession*), is a particularly comforting and consoling sacrament because if we are sorry for our sins,[1] we are able to confess them with our own lips and then hear with our own ears that God has forgiven us. How else could we know that we have been forgiven by God? This sacrament, when worthily received, assures us that our sins are forgiven. We do not have to rely on a subjective "feeling." In other words, if we confess all our sins with sorrow and receive absolution, we can be certain that we are on the right path to Heaven. Even though the Biblical basis of this sacrament is very clear,[2] some people are inclined to think, "When Christ gave His apostles the power to forgive sins did He *really* institute this sacrament? How could God in all of His mercy ask us to do something so difficult?" But it is precisely because God *is* merciful that He has given us this sacrament. He understands how much we need to *know* that we are forgiven.

---

[1] For a basic definition of sin see *Appendix A*.

[2] See *Appendix B*.

The Church teaches that we even receive pardon for the serious sins we forget to confess.[1] However, were we to recollect them, we must confess them the next time we go to confession. In the meantime, we may receive Holy Communion, if no other obstacle presents itself.[2] The only things which make this sacrament invalid are intentionally withholding serious sins,[3] not being sorry for them, or not having a *firm purpose of amendment.* The *purpose* of amendment is not the *certitude* of amendment but a sincere resolve, with the help of God's grace, not to sin again and to avoid what leads us to sin.

Questions for Personal Reflection or Group Discussion

Read *Appendix A.* Has the answer to the question, "What is Sin?" helped you to view sin any differently?

Do you think Catholics are fortunate or unfortunate in having the Sacrament of Reconciliation? Why?

---

[1] cf. *Council of Trent,* Session XIV, ch. 5.

[2] cf. Rev Heribert Jone, OFM Cap, JCD, *Moral Theology*, 18th ed. (Westminster, 1962), no. 564, p. 400.

[3] cf. *Council of Trent,* Session XIV, ch. 5. We will have a closer look at what constitutes a serious sin in chapter four.

Chapter Two

Reconciliation with God

Friends who truly value each other long to be reconciled whenever they have offended one another. It is the same with our friendship with Christ. Even those who only have a small amount of faith are able to recognise that God's love is something that they would not want to offend or take for granted.

Being reconciled to God is a benefit that we can appreciate even more if we consider it from God's point of view. Often we only think of the Sacrament of Reconciliation in terms of what *we* want from it, namely, to receive God's pardon and peace. But have you ever considered what *God* wants? He wants us to be reconciled to Himself *before* we even want to be forgiven. Have you also considered that He wants to lavish His love upon us when we return, even if we have offended Him grievously? These are indeed God's desires, for in the *Parable of the Prodigal Son* Jesus said that while the son (who represents us when we are seeking God's mercy) was on his way back to his father (who represents God) but "was yet at a distance, his father saw him and had compassion, and ran and embraced him and kissed him."[1] Notice how the father was not waiting in the comfort of his home. If he was able to see his son returning while he was "*yet at a distance*" he must have been 'scanning the horizons' for the first sign of his son's return.

---

[1] Lk 15:20.

Perhaps we would not take God's mercy for granted so much if we consider what the father did *not* say. There is not a hint of him saying anything such as, "You have hurt me very much. You have a hide to be coming back. What makes you think you can start all over again? I do not know what I can do to help you. It is going to take me a long time to forgive you." On the contrary, there was no harbouring of hurt, no resentment – only intense joy. By returning to his father the prodigal son could not have done anything more to please him. Likewise, of all the ways we can please God, nothing exceeds going to Confession. Heaven itself gives testimony to this claim: "I tell you," said Jesus, "there will be more joy in heaven over one sinner who repents than over ninety-nine righteous persons who need no repentance."[2]

The intensity of the father's desire to forgive his son was not diminished, but increased by his restless waiting. He was restless because he knew that he could not bully his son into returning. Nor could he forgive him until his son asked for forgiveness. So when we return to God in the Sacrament of Reconciliation, as did the prodigal son, can you imagine how much God our loving Father is happy to restore us to the dignity of what it is to be His children if it has been lost? If we have not committed a serious sin, Christ nevertheless extends the warmth of His embrace and brings us closer to Himself. This benefit is indeed a beautiful one, especially when we consider that His presence is mediated sacramentally through the ministry of the priest as we shall see in the next chapter.

[2] Lk 15:7.

Questions for Personal Reflection or Group Discussion

Do you think going to Confession is easier if you consider what happens in this sacrament from God's point of view?

What do you think of the statement, "Of all the ways we can please God, nothing exceeds going to Confession"?

The *Parable of the Prodigal Son* contains many good things to contemplate. Is there anything else about this parable which touches you?

THE GIFT OF CONFESSION

Chapter Three

Personal Encounter with Christ

As comforting as it is to know that our sins are forgiven in Confession, this is not the only reason why Christ gave us this sacrament. He gave it to us so that we could have a *personal encounter* with Him. Although we encounter Christ in all the sacraments, He meets our own individual and particular need for mercy in this sacrament. Divine mercy is experienced in numerous ways, but it reaches it highest intensity and finds its most eloquent expression at the moment when we kneel before Christ represented in the priest to ask for forgiveness.

A Greater Joy than Pardon and Peace

Knowing that we are encountering Christ in this sacrament is a benefit that far outweighs the difficulties involved in confessing our sins. It even outweighs the joy of knowing that our sins are forgiven. The encounter with Christ that the woman at the well had in St John's Gospel demonstrates this. Since Jesus had gained her trust, she felt comfortable to open her heart and acknowledge her sins. In doing so, she was deeply touched by His mercy, understanding, and compassion. She then went into the city and brought back with her a number of men so that she could introduce them to Him. She did this not just because she had her sins forgiven, but because she had met Christ and now wanted others to be able to encounter Him too.[1] Her

[1] cf. Jn 4:1-42.

experience is available to all Catholics because the Sacrament of Holy Orders enables priests to "become living instruments of Christ the eternal priest … every priest in his own way represents the person of Christ Himself."[2] Jesus said to St Faustina Kowalska:

> *When you approach the confessional, know this, that I Myself am waiting there for you. I am only hidden by the priest, but I Myself act in your soul. Here the misery of the soul meets the God of mercy.*[3]

My Encounter with Christ as a Penitent

As a penitent, I personally encounter Christ in ways that constantly surprise me. It seems too good to be true that the "bad news" of my sins can be exchanged for the Good News of Christ, namely, His assurance that He still loves me unconditionally and that He wants to heal, strengthen, encourage and make me more like Himself. There is no "raw deal" in that marvellous exchange! This encounter does not simply take place in the exchange of words themselves, because the tone of his voice, together with all the other characteristics of his demeanor, also convey Christ's compassionate and non-judgmental understanding. The more transparent I am, the more "transparent" the priest is; transparent in the sense that I can "see through" him and recognise Christ! Since Jesus said, "He who has seen me has seen the Father,"[4] this encounter puts me in touch with what it is to be loved by God the Father.

Then, when He places His hand over my head to invoke the Holy Spirit down upon me, I am comforted and consoled. It is such a tangible affirmation of His love for in this gesture I am moved by the reality that it is Christ who is reaching out to reunite me to Himself. In this I do not just perceive Christ's presence, but what He is actively doing within my heart, that is, transforming me so that my desires are more centered on Him. Finally, I am always uplifted when I hear Christ say through the priest, "I absolve you from your sins," especially when I am ashamed by my own weaknesses, for His mercy enables me to see myself more in relation to His capacity to forgive than my personal sense of failure.

---

[2] Vatican Council II, *Decree on the Ministry and Life of Priests (Presbyterorum Ordinis),* no. 12.

[3] *Divine Mercy in my Soul: Diary of Sister M. Faustina Kowalska*, (Stockbridge,1990), no.1602.

[4] Jn 14:9.

It naturally follows that Christ's presence which is mediated through the ministry of the priest is something that I find immensely fulfilling and rewarding. Since encountering Christ is so ennobling, I always find myself being able to follow Him with a stronger faith, a more fervent love, and a renewed hope and confidence in Him. None of this happens to the same extent before I go to Confession. Sure, Christ can be encountered anywhere, but I find that His presence is never as tangible and touching as where He has requested Himself to be found. It surprises me to hear people say that they have a "personal relationship" with Christ and yet choose to relate to Him in ways which are impersonal by avoiding the sacraments. This is contradictory, especially when we consider that Christ Himself gave us the sacraments so that we can encounter Him in a personal way.

Some people argue that you could still encounter Christ if you received absolution without having to confess your sins.[5] This argument initially sounds convincing because it appeals to the natural difficulties involved in disclosing them, but it overlooks how the confession of sins is integral to the Sacrament of Reconciliation. Despite this, people often ask, "Why do I need to confess my sins to a priest?" On this point, *Appendix B* may be of interest, as it contains assuring answers to this and other frequently asked questions which arise from the difficulties involved in going to Confession.

The Seal of Confession

Since the Church teaches that Christ is encountered in this sacrament through the ministry of the priest, it follows that your confession is only between you and God. This is why the priest is bound by what is called the *Seal of Confession* by which you are assured that he will not, in any circumstance whatsoever (i) tell anyone the contents of your confession; (ii) let anyone know what penance he has given you; (iii) act upon any of the information he learned from your confession; and (iv) speak to you about your sins outside the confessional. For example, if a priest saw

[5] *Absolution* comes from the Latin word, "*absolvere*," meaning, "*to loose*" or "*to free*." It is the moment within this sacrament when Christ forgives the penitent through the ministry of the Church and the words of absolution as the priest extends his hands or at least his right hand over the penitent's head.

you on the street he could not say, "Oh, did you ever pay back the money you stole?"

Even if a priest is asked to break the Seal of Confession by the highest of civil jurisdictions, he is not permitted to do so by the Church.[6] If a priest directly violates this Seal he incurs, there and then, an automatic excommunication[7] and the only one who can reinstate him in union with the Church is the pope. *Appendix D* contains some true stories of priests who remained faithful to the seal. Such stories not only help penitents to have a greater confidence in Confession, they also provide no shortage of inspiration to priests in their desire to represent Christ faithfully in this sacrament.

Questions for Personal Reflection or Group Discussion

Describe the way you personally encounter Christ in the Sacrament of Reconciliation.

Read *Appendix C*. Have the answers to these frequently asked questions about Confession helped you to have a renewed appreciation for this sacrament?

Has learning how humbling it is for priests to represent Christ in Confession helped you to be less anxious?

If God is calling you to the Priesthood, but a sense of unworthiness is stopping you from responding, does it encourage you to think that the awareness of your own weaknesses could actually help you to be a good priest?

Have you ever had a negative experience of Confession? If so, what did you do to not let it discourage you?

---

[6] cf. *Rite of Penance*, no.10d; *CIC*, can. 983, §1.

[7] cf. *CIC*, can.1388, §1.

Chapter Four

Divine Life is Restored in our Soul (Spiritual Resurrection)

As we will see in chapter five, mortal sin results in the *loss of sanctifying grace*. If a person commits this kind of sin he is said to be no longer in the *state of grace* which means that God's divine life ceases to dwell within him. That many are not aware of this suggests that there is a widespread unawareness of how necessary and how precious God's divine life is to us. St Teresa of Avila said that "the soul of the just person is nothing else but a paradise where the Lord says He finds His delight."[1] We anticipate Heaven to be our paradise. But the Lord considers His "paradise" to be "the soul of the just person," that is, a soul that is united to Him. Surely the Lord wishes this delight He experiences to be reciprocated, that we take pleasure in knowing that God dwells within us, and that we try to restore His divine life in our soul when it is lost through sin. Upon contemplating this St Teresa said:

> *Because we have heard and because faith tells us so, we know we have souls. But we seldom consider the precious things that can be found in this soul, or who dwells within it, or its high value. Consequently, little effort is made to preserve its beauty.*[2]

Furthermore, Pope Pius XII said that "the sin of the age is the loss of the sense of sin."[3] Today sensitivity towards sin has not only been lost, rather, sin is sometimes even glorified. In light of this, if the ignorance of the reality of sin was less widespread, more Catholics would have a better appreciation for the Sacrament of Reconciliation. So to that end, let us have a closer look at sin, especially mortal sin because it separates

---

[1] *The Interior Castle,* I, ch. 1, no. 1.

[2] *Ibid,* no. 2.

[3] Radio Message to the US National Catechetical Congress in Boston (26 October 1946): Discorsi e Radiomessaggi VIII, 288.

us from God. By definition, a mortal sin (otherwise known as serious or grave sin) must involve *all three* of the following conditions:

- *(i)* *serious matter*;
- *(ii)* *sufficient knowledge* (sufficient reflection that the thought, word, action, or omission at hand is seriously sinful) ; and
- *(iii)* *deliberate consent* (consent sufficiently deliberate to be a personal choice.)

Since each of these conditions has their own complexities, we would do well to take a closer look at them:

Serious Matter

Serious matter pertains to a *major violation* of any one of the *Ten Commandments*. Although all serious matter is embodied in these commands God gave through Moses, we often need to refer to other parts of Scripture and to the Church's teachings for a more comprehensive understanding of what constitutes serious matter because the Ten Commandments are only a basic moral guide. Hence it can be helpful to know that serious matter also pertains to the following:

- Seriously failing to observe any of the *Precepts of the Church*.[4]
- Committing one of the *Sins that Cry out to Heaven*.[5] These are wilful murder (cf. Gen 4:10), the sin of Sodom (cf. Gen 18:20), oppression of the poor (cf. Ex 2:23), and defrauding labourers of their wages (cf. Jam 5:4.)
- Sinning against the *theological virtues* of faith, hope and charity in a major way is serious matter because these virtues ultimately have God as their object. To give a few examples, it is serious matter for

---

[4] See *Appendix E*.

[5] cf. *Catechism of the Catholic Church (CCC)*, no.1867.

a person to sin against *faith* by obstinately and purposely teaching heresy (something contrary to what has been revealed by God.) Likewise, it is serious matter to sin against *hope* either by *presumption* or *despair*. Presumption occurs when a person presumes that he will receive God's forgiveness for a serious sin without repentance. Despair consists in a wilful failure to hope or believe in God's mercy. It is also serious matter if a person purposely sins against *charity* by refusing to help someone in serious need when he has the opportunity and the means to do so.[6]

- St Paul provides us with other sins which constitute serious matter:

> *fornication [sex outside of marriage], impurity, licentiousness, idolatry, sorcery, enmity, strife, jealousy, anger, selfishness, dissension, party spirit [divisive factions], envy, drunkenness, carousing [riotous behaviour], and the like. I warn you, as I warned you before, that those who do such things shall not inherit the kingdom of God.*[7]

Naturally, St Paul is not suggesting that the emotions and desires above always constitute serious matter because our feelings and urges are not sinful in and of themselves. In fact, it can be meritorious to overcome violent temptations to be impure, angry, or envious for example. But when a person's desires become seriously disordered, or when he allows his emotions to carry over into a word, action, or omission that hurts someone grievously, only then would they constitute serious matter. What can be said about St Paul's list of sins above also applies to what the Church calls the *Capital Sins*, which are also understood to be sources of serious matter. These are serious sins of pride, greed, envy, anger, lust, gluttony, and laziness.[8]

Further explanation of what serious matter consists of is found in the following example: A person who plucks a few grapes and eats them while shopping in a grocery store has broken the Seventh Commandment, "You shall not steal." But such a sin does not involve serious matter because it is only a *minor* violation of this Commandment. On the other

[6] cf. *CCC*, nos. 2088-89, 2091, 2094.

[7] Gal 5:19-21. Other sins which constitute serious matter are mentioned in 1 Cor 5:11; 6:9; Eph 4:17:19; Col 3:1-9; 2 Tim 3:2-7; and 2 Pet 2:1-3, 12-14, 19.

[8] cf. *CCC*, no. 1866.

hand, if someone stole enough grapes from a shop or vineyard that would have an impact on the owner's livelihood, this would be a *major* violation of this Commandment and thus it would constitute serious matter. Furthermore, since a major violation is determined by the harm it causes, stealing a loaf of bread from the average family home would not constitute serious matter, whereas stealing bread from a poor and destitute person would.

Serious matter can also be *indirectly* related to the Ten Commandments. Jesus made this clear when He said:

> *You have heard that it was said to the men of old, "You shall not kill; and whoever kills shall be liable to judgment." But I say to you that every one who is angry with his brother shall be liable to judgment; whoever insults his brother shall be liable to the council, and whoever says, "You fool!" shall be liable to the hell of fire.*[9]

In other words, a person who has inflicted bodily harm on another person, or has engaged in, or threatened someone with physical, verbal, or emotional abuse has violated the Fifth Commandment, "You shall not kill" in a major way, even though he has not actually killed him. That Jesus said such a person is "liable to the hell of fire" leaves no question about how serious matter is not *exclusive* to what is stated in the Ten Commandments per se. Of course, if the bodily harm or abuse in this instance is not grievous it would only be a minor violation of this Commandment.

As for blasphemy, however, this constitutes serious matter even when the Second Commandment, "You shall not take the name of the Lord your God in vain," is violated in a minor way. Blasphemy, however small, is always serious matter because it constitutes a direct contempt for the infinite majesty of God Himself.[10] Likewise, the Church has consistently taught that minor violations against the Sixth and Ninth Commandments (directly willed[11] sexual pleasure in thought, word, or action outside of marriage) always involve serious matter.[12] We owe this

[9] Mt 5:21-22.

[10] cf. *CCC,* no. 2148.

[11] As opposed to *indirectly* willed or *involuntary* sexual activity such as nocturnal emissions.

[12] "According to Christian and Church teaching and as right reason acknowledges sexual morality encompasses such important human values that every violation of it is objectively grave." (Congregation of the Doctrine of the Faith, *Declaration on Certain Questions Concerning Sexual Ethics (Persona humana),* 1975, no.10).

understanding to what Jesus said to those who considered that impure thoughts do not constitute serious matter:

> *You have heard that it was said, "You shall not commit adultery." But I say to you that every one who looks at a woman lustfully has already committed adultery with her in his heart.*[13]

For this reason the Holy Office said, "In actions of impurity there is no light matter."[14] Engaging in foreplay in order to arouse passion reserved for marriage is also serious matter if it is not part of a marital act.[15] There is no cause for alarm if this happens without knowingly intending it, for as we shall see below, serious matter does not always constitute mortal sin; it must also involve sufficient knowledge and deliberate consent. Notwithstanding this, if a person considered that sins against purity are only a minor violation of the Sixth and Ninth Commandments he would be overlooking that (i) the Bible clearly teaches that directly willed sexual activity belongs in marriage alone;[16] (ii) our human sexuality is an extraordinary gift by which God has made us in His image;[17] (iii) our bodies are temples of the Holy Spirit;[18] and (iv) our sexuality is "by no means something purely biological, but concerns the innermost being of the human person."[19]

Sufficient Knowledge and Deliberate Consent

Committing a mortal sin is not like breaking a taboo because to sin we have to *know* that what we are doing is morally wrong. This is why a mortal sin cannot be committed without *sufficient knowledge* that the thought, word, action, or omission at hand is seriously sinful. Likewise, it could never be said that a mortal sin is committed by accident because it cannot be committed without *deliberate consent.* Sufficient knowledge and deliberate consent can sometimes be diminished and/or inhibited by ignorance, immaturity, fear, depression, psychological imbalance, trauma

---

[13] Mt 5:27-28.

[14] *Response of the Holy Office,*11 Feb 1561 (*DS* 2013). See also *CCC,* no. 2352.

[15] cf. Pope Alexander VII, 1666, (*DS* 2060).

[16] cf. Ex 20:14; Deut 5:18; Mt 15:19; 19:18; Rom 13:9; Col 3:5; Eph 5:3.

[17] cf. Gen 1:26-28.

[18] cf. 1 Cor 3:16-17; 6:19-20; 2 Cor 6:16.

[19] John Paul II, *The Role of the Christian Family in the Modern World (Familiaris Consortio),* no. 11. See also *CCC,* no. 2332.

from being abused, anger, coercion, compulsion, passion, substance addiction and the force of habit. These mitigating circumstances and emotions can make a person less culpable. Notwithstanding this, factors which diminish sufficient knowledge and deliberate consent do not necessarily vitiate them altogether. The absence of serious responsibility must not be presumed as this would be to misunderstand the moral capacity of the human person.

As we can see, while this definition of mortal sin enables us to judge the sin it never allows us to judge the sinner because only God knows whether or not all three of these conditions were actually present when a person did something morally wrong. Sometimes it can be hard enough to judge whether we have violated one of the Commandments in a major way or not ourselves.

Our awareness of these complexities gives us further reason to be grateful for the Sacrament of Reconciliation. In confessing our sins as *dubious* (being uncertain of their gravity) we have the opportunity to ask the priest to shed light on our uncertainties. He is not infallible, but by drawing on the Church's doctrine and spiritual tradition he can provide valuable advice. Since we can sometimes erroneously accuse ourselves of mortal sin this can be particularly helpful, without which we would lack much interior peace. At this point we are not considering *venial sin*[20] for it is a sin which St John said does not lead to death: "there is sin which is not mortal."[21] But St John does say, "There is sin which is mortal".[22] What St John says here helps us to correct a common misunderstanding[23], namely, the misguided assertion, "There is no such thing as mortal sin." Commenting upon these words of St John, Pope John Paul II said:

> *Obviously, the concept of death here is a spiritual death. It is a question of the loss of the true life or "eternal life," which for John is knowledge of the Father and the Son, (cf. 1 Jn 17:3) and communion and intimacy with them.*[24]

[20] "*Venial*" comes from the Latin word meaning, "*pardonable*." Venial sins consist of a minor violation of the Commandments, or a failure to meet the requirements of God's law in a less serious matter. It can also consist of a major violation of the Commandments committed *without* sufficient knowledge or deliberate consent (cf. *CCC*, no.1862).

[21] 1Jn 5:17.

[22] 1Jn 5:16.

[23] *Appendix C* contains three other common misunderstandings of what constitutes mortal sin.

In reminding us of this reality, Pope John Paul II reaffirmed the teaching of the Council of Trent concerning the existence and nature of mortal sin.[25] Among those who do acknowledge its reality, some argue that it only consists in such things as premeditated murder, that it is very rare, and that only depraved and very evil people commit this kind of sin. But if you refer to the examination of conscience in *Appendix F,* you will realise that mortal sin can be more common than that. On the other hand, it is not the kind of sin by which the righteous man falls seven times a day as depicted in the Book of Proverbs.[26] Nevertheless, the Church teaches that "mortal sin is a radical possibility of human freedom, as is love itself."[27]

The Effects of Mortal Sin

The Church teaches that when a person knowingly and willingly violates God's Commandments he not only rejects God's law but he rejects God Himself. A mortal sin thereby breaks our covenant and communion with God, deprives us of sanctifying grace, God's friendship, charity, and consequently eternal happiness.[28] In short, mortal sin "kills" the divine life within the soul. Just as a body without a soul is dead, a soul without sanctifying grace is dead. This is why a sin of this kind is called "mortal." As we shall see, this term does *not* mean God's divine life cannot be restored in the soul in the same way the human body cannot be restored to life if it sustains a mortal wound. This unhappy parallel in calling such sins "mortal" is no doubt why many people find this term unpleasant.

Notwithstanding this, while this kind of sin does not immediately lead to *physical* death it certainly brings about an immediate *spiritual* death which remains until repentance and reconciliation with God. That is why Christ asked St John to write to the church in Sardis, "I know all about you: how you are reputed to be alive and yet are dead."[29] In the *Parable of the Prodigal Son,* Jesus Himself describes serious sin as a spiritual death, for in speaking to the elder brother, the father says, "your brother here was dead and has come to life; he was lost and is found."[30]

---

[24] *Reconciliatio et Paenitentia,* no. 17.
[25] cf. *Ibid,* no. 17.
[26] cf. Prov 24:16.
[27] *CCC,* no. 1861.
[28] cf. *CCC,* nos. 1472, 1861.

Spiritual Resurrection

Being able to understand mortal sin for what it is means that we will less likely take for granted another great benefit that the Sacrament of Reconciliation provides. That is, our soul is brought back to life in Christ, for as St Paul said, "You were dead, because you were sinners ... but he [Christ] has brought you to life with him, he has forgiven us all our sins."[31] Upon this Dr Scott Hahn makes a poignant observation. He says, "If doctors could do for our bodies what priests can do for our souls [that is, restore life when it is lost] they would be worked to death!" Being brought back to life in Christ means that (i) our covenant with God is restored; (ii) we are sanctified with the grace that enables us to participate in His eternal, divine life and His charity; (iii) the Holy Trinity dwells within us; and (iv) our friendship with God is restored. This is by no means a trivial benefit we receive from the Sacrament of Reconciliation. It can only be seen as trivial by those who trivialise mortal sin itself.

---

[29] Rev 3:1. (*JB*)
[30] Lk15:32. (*JB*)
[31] Col 2:13. See also Rom 6:13; Eph 2:1, 5; 5:14.

Questions for Personal Reflection or Group Discussion

Do you agree with the statement Pope Pius XII made about the loss of the sense of sin? Why or why not?

What do you think of Dr Scott Hahn's statement, "If doctors could do for our bodies what priests can do for our souls they would be worked to death!"?

Chapter Five

God's Grace is Given

The word "*grace*" occurs repeatedly in the New Testament. It appears about a hundred and fifty times. It comes from the Greek word "*charis,*" meaning "*favour*" or "*gift.*" We often think of Confession only in terms of what it takes away, namely sin, but this sacrament also provides us with *sanctifying grace* and *sacramental grace.*

Sanctifying Grace

Since life in Heaven is "*supernatural*" (that is, "*above nature*") we need supernatural means to get there. Trying to get to Heaven without God's help is just as impossible as trying to fly to the moon without a rocket! This supernatural assistance we understand to be *sanctifying grace.* This special gift is called "sanctifying" grace because it unites us to the Sanctifier, God Himself. ("*Sanctify*" means to "*make holy.*") If we committed a mortal sin, sanctifying grace re-unites us to Him. It thereby enables us to intimately share in God's own divine life as His children. This means that we are restored to the grace we received in the Sacrament of Baptism. If we deprive ourselves of sanctifying grace we are not totally depriving ourselves of God's help because God never withholds *actual graces* from us which help us to repent, avoid evil and do good. Unlike sanctifying grace, however, actual graces do not unite us to God if our union with Him has been lost through mortal sin.

Jesus gives us further insight into the necessity of sanctifying grace in the *Parable of the Ten Bridesmaids.* The five foolish bridesmaids were not able to enter the marriage feast because they had no oil in their lamps. Consequently, Jesus said to them, "Truly, I say to you, I do not know you."[1] To this you may ask, "But God knows everything and everyone. He knows us better than we know ourselves. Why then did He not know them?" It all goes back to their lamps; the five foolish bridesmaids had no oil in them. No oil, no flame. Perhaps Jesus gave this parable to illustrate how important His grace is. As we have seen, mortal sins extinguish sanctifying grace in the soul. A lamp deprived of oil is analogous to a soul deprived of grace – just as a flame cannot remain present in a lamp without oil, God cannot remain present in a soul without sanctifying grace.

Now consider that what makes us loveable in the Father's eyes more than anything else is that He can behold His own Beloved Son within us. It follows that God (who is Father, Son, and Holy Spirit) cannot recognise Himself in a soul deprived of sanctifying grace. So if Christ does not dwell in a soul, there is every reason for God to say to him, as He did to the five foolish bridesmaids, "I do not know you." However, since the Sacrament of Reconciliation replenishes sanctifying grace in our soul if it has been lost, it has the beautiful effect of enabling God our Father to behold, embrace, and cherish us as He does His own Beloved Son!

As for how much sanctifying grace is given, St Thomas Aquinas said that since the effects of Confession are always in proportion to the excellence of our dispositions with which we receive this sacrament, we have the opportunity to arise to an even greater grace than that which we had before we sinned, as was the case with Mary Magdalene.[2] Even when we only have venial sins to confess and are already in the state of grace, with the proper dispositions, sanctifying grace is increased within us. In this sense we can see that the Sacrament of Reconciliation gives us much more than it takes away. We have the opportunity to be filled with grace in a manner depicted by St Paul, "where sin increased, grace abounded all the more."[3]

As we receive sanctifying grace God also restores and/or strengthens within us the *gifts of the Holy Spirit* and the *supernatural virtues* (we will look at these more closely in chapter thirteen). Our *intellect* (the faculty we have by which we are able to know and reason) is enlightened by Christ who

---

[1] Mt 25:12.

[2] cf. *Summa Theologica,* III, q.89, a.2.

[3] Rom 5:20.

is the Truth itself; our *will* (the faculty we have by which we are able to choose and love) is strengthened in its resolve to follow and love Christ; and our *body* becomes His temple.

When sanctifying grace comes into our intellect it enlightens it with the gift of *faith*. How does it enlighten? Fulton Sheen gives a number of analogies to help us see how. The gift of faith is like what a telescope is to the eye. It does not destroy the eye, it perfects it. It gives it new vision, a new certitude, quite beyond reason, enabling us to believe everything that God has revealed. For example, it is beyond reason to believe that God is three Persons, but one God. However, since God has revealed this, through faith we are able to believe it. We have the same eyes at night as we have in the day, but we do not see at night because we lack the light of the sun. Since Confession restores and/or increases the light of the sun (sanctifying grace according to this analogy), it enables us to grow in our knowledge of God and to see life from a new perspective. This in turn provides us with a new outlook on birth, suffering, death, joy, happiness, knowing right from wrong, and all the other aspects of life.

The gift of faith does not *contradict* reason as some people allege. Rather, faith *perfects* reason, enabling us to see truths that we could not see on our own. When a person gets drunk he loses much of his power to reason. Do his senses function well? Does he see well? Does he walk well? Does he speak well? Why do his senses not work well? Because the effect of alcohol has diminished his ability to reason. In the same way, when the effect of sin diminishes a person's faith, his ability to reason is less perfect. Conversely, just as our *senses* are perfected by reason, our *reason* is perfected by faith.

It is interesting to read the writings of those who once had faith and lost it. When their faith was strong their writings contained no shortage of inspiration due to the logic and clarity of thought with which they wrote. But if we read what they wrote after they had lost their faith, it portrays minds that are wandering and confused. This suggests that reason does not exercise itself as well without faith as with it.[4] Such comparisons

[4] cf. Fulton J. Sheen, *Your Life is Worth Living* (Schnecksville, 2001), pp. 173, 190.

and observations help us to see how wonderful is the gift of faith which we receive when sanctifying grace comes into our minds.

When sanctifying grace comes into the will it strengthens it to resist temptation and to grow in virtue. This thereby increases within us the virtue of *hope* by which we are able to trust that following Christ (even though this may be difficult at times) will lead to our own happiness on earth and eternal happiness in Heaven. Sanctifying grace also strengthens our will like a fan which intensifies the flames of a fire, restoring and/or increasing within us the virtue of *charity* (otherwise known as *love*.) Confession thereby enables us to love God above all things, and our neighbours as ourselves for His own sake.

It can also be helpful to know how this sacrament restores and increases the theological virtues of faith, hope and love not only in theory but in practice. This we will look at in chapters fifteen to seventeen.

Sacramental Grace

Sacramental grace helps us not only to avoid evil but to do good. It provides us with the special help we need (i) to avoid relapsing into the sins we have just confessed; (ii) to struggle against the temptations that lead to them; and (iii) it even increases our ability to encounter Christ in the midst of any subsequent temptations, an encounter that enables the very weaknesses we have to lead us closer to Him. Little wonder that Christ told St Paul, "my power is made perfect in weakness."[5] This reality is clearly evident to those who regularly confess their sins.

On this topic, Jesus told St Faustina some encouraging words: "I desire to grant unimaginable graces to those who trust in my mercy."[6] On another occasion He said:

> *Daughter, when you go to confession, to this fountain of My mercy, the Blood and Water which came forth from My Heart always flows down upon your soul and ennobles it. Every time you go to confession, immerse yourself entirely in My mercy, with great trust, so that I may pour the bounty of My grace upon your soul.*[7]

[5] 2 Cor 12:9.

[6] *Divine Mercy in my Soul: Diary of Sister M. Faustina Kowalska*, no.687.

[7] *Ibid*, no. 1602.

Questions for Personal Reflection or Group Discussion

Does it help to consider that by giving us grace, the Sacrament of Reconciliation gives us much more than it takes away?

How have you experienced the effects of God's grace in your life?

Chapter Six

It Reminds Us of the Price of Sin

Perhaps the best way of appreciating what Christ does for us in the Sacrament of Reconciliation is to contemplate the mercy He showed to the woman caught in adultery. Jesus was asked by the Pharisees if she should be stoned to death or not. He responded by saying, "Let him who is without sin among you be the first to throw a stone at her."[1] His answer is as wise as it is famous, as it saved her from death. But what about Jesus? Why did He not throw the first stone? He said only the innocent may condemn, and He is sinless. The Law of Moses declared that an adulterous woman had to be stoned to death.[2] Since this sacred Law was "the work of God, and the writing [on the tablets of stone] was the writing of God,"[3] would not Jesus be contradicting Himself if He disobeyed that Law?

This question becomes more confounding when you consider that Jesus said, "Think not that I have come to abolish the law and the prophets; I have come not to abolish them but to fulfil them."[4] How could Jesus bestow mercy upon this woman and yet still fulfil the Law? How could He reconcile her to Himself if He could not reconcile mercy with justice? Jesus was a man of justice, so why did He not condemn her? Because, as Fulton Sheen said, Jesus would be condemned for her. And for us too! By not stoning her, He was not making light of sin, because on the Cross He would assume its burden. He was not overlooking the injustice of her sin, for His Passion

[1] Jn 8:7.
[2] cf. Lev 20:10.
[3] Ex 32:16.
[4] Mt 5:17.

and Death would satisfy divine justice.[5] The Prophet Isaiah had foretold this centuries before: "He has borne our griefs and carried our sorrows ... he was wounded for our transgressions, he was bruised for our iniquities; upon him was the chastisement that made us whole, and with his stripes we are healed ... and the Lord has laid on him the iniquity of us all ... he shall bear their iniquities."[6]

The following true story also illustrates how Confession reminds us of what Christ has done to restore us to His friendship. A number of boys in a gang wandered into a church. They could see people lining up to go to Confession. Being a rather devious lot, they dared each other to make a mockery of those who were confessing their sins. So they went in and made fun of the people, causing great disturbance among them. They began to swear at them and make fun of confessing their sins, while one of them went right up onto the sanctuary and knelt before the Crucifix. Looking up to Christ on the Cross, he clenched his fist and shouted, "You died for me. Well I don't give a..." He could not finish what he was prepared to say. He was so moved by the love of Christ – so much so – that when this boy grew up, he entered the Priesthood and is now a bishop!

Questions for Personal Reflection or Group Discussion

Do you think Jesus' response to the woman caught in adultery would have profoundly changed her life?

We contemplate Christ's Passion and Death in the Sacrifice of the Mass and in popular devotions, such as the Stations of the Cross and the Rosary. How often do you also contemplate Christ's Crucifixion in association with the Sacrament of Reconciliation?

---

[5] cf. *Life of Christ* (New York, 1977), p.188.

[6] Isa 53:4-6, 11 (Emphasis added).

Chapter Seven

The Profits of Penance

Reparation

The penance the priest prescribes (which usually consists of prayer, good works, and/or self-denial) enables us to repair in some measure the harm we have caused to any particular person(s) and to the whole of Christ's Mystical Body (the Church is called Christ's "*Mystical Body*" because in a mysterious way it is Christ Himself.) In order to understand why our sins harm the Mystical Body of Christ it can be helpful to see how Christ and His Church are united in one body. Christ is the head of the Church.[1] This Church consists of the People of God. Christ identifies Himself as our "bridegroom"[2] who is uniting Himself to us, His bride, such that the two become one body.

How closely united in one body are we? Just as your head would cry out if I stepped on your foot, when Saul persecuted the Christians (the members of Christ's Mystical Body), Christ (the head of the Mystical Body) cried out to him from Heaven, "Saul, Saul, why do you persecute me?"[3] The Church is not just a mere human institution because notice how Christ did not say, "Why are you persecuting my followers?" Rather, He said, "Why do you persecute *me*?" Christ is identifying Himself so closely with His Church that to persecute His followers is to persecute *Him* – Personally. This is consistent with what Christ said to His disciples: "Truly, I say to you, as you did it to one of the least of these my brethren, you did it to me."[4] St Paul provides

[1] cf. Col 1:18; 2:9, 19; Eph 1:10, 22-23; 4:15-16; 5:23.
[2] cf. Mt 9:15; Mk 2:19; Lk 5:34; Rev 19:7.
[3] Acts 9:4; 22:7; 26:4.

further insight into how the afflictions of Christ and His Church are one and the same:

> *Now I rejoice in my sufferings for your sake, and in my flesh I complete what is lacking in Christ's afflictions for the sake of his body, that is, the Church.*[5]

Is there anything *lacking* in Christ's Passion and Death? Was Christ's suffering insufficient to redeem and purify us completely? While it is *sufficient for all*, it is not *all efficient.* That is, Christ's suffering was *objectively* sufficient for our salvation, but not *subjectively* because due to attachment to sin and human weakness, not every Christian does penance. This is why St Paul said that his sufferings help to "complete what is lacking in Christ's afflictions." The "afflictions" of Christ he is referring to here are not those the Person of Christ has undergone once and for all, but the afflictions Christ continues to undergo in the members of His Mystical Body, the Church. Since Christ is afflicted in this sense, St Paul deems reparation to be necessary.

Sharing in Christ's Redemptive Work

Although Christ's physical body is in the glory of Heaven, Christ's Mystical Body is not yet completely redeemed. This means that as Christ (the head) suffered for the Church (the members of His Mystical Body), so we are called to incorporate our own sacrifices into His by participating in His Passion. This is not unlike creation. God created the world, but in putting it into our hands, we as its stewards have to complete it with our technology, arts and sciences.[6] In doing so, we are participating in God's *creative* power. Likewise, by applying our own sacrifices to Christ's Sacrifice we are participating in His *redemptive* power, for as St Paul said: "We are God's fellow workers."[7]

It follows that when we do our penance out of love for Christ and out of sorrow for having offended Him, we thereby become more sensitive to how we are called not only to make reparation for the harm we have done to Christ, but also to the members of His Mystical Body,

[4] Mt 25:40.
[5] Col 1:24.
[6] cf. Gen 1:26, 28-30.
[7] cf. 1 Cor 3:9.

the Church. The Sacrament of Penance thereby helps us to see that we could never say, "Sin is just a 'personal matter' between me and God." Some people think that sins such as missing Mass on a Sunday, using God's name in vain, impure thoughts and actions, gluttony, etc, are not so bad because unlike other sins, these do not harm anyone else. As we have seen, however, this is not true. Every kind of sin – including those that do not seem to harm anyone else – injures the Mystical Body of Christ. This means that all of our brothers and sisters in Christ *are* affected.

This is the main reason why we are given some penance in this sacrament. This Mystery is also known as the "communion of saints."[8] The word "*communion*" is significant here because when "*com*" (the Latin word for "*with*") and "*union*" are put together they form a word which expresses the nature of our union with Christ. Since we are members of His Mystical Body, being united to Christ means that we are thereby united *with* one another in Him.

Incidentally, this is why the Church says that the priest not only acts on behalf of Christ in Confession, but also on behalf of the Church, because being reconciled with Christ means we are also being reconciled with one another. This has benefits of its own. Take a person who offends someone but due to an inability to ever meet that person again, he is unable to apologise to him. His need to say, "Sorry" is fulfilled in Confession because the priest is called not only to "fill the shoes" of Christ, but also the "shoes" of our brothers and sisters who are members of the Mystical Body of Christ. Likewise, the penitent has an opportunity to repair the harm he has done to that person by fulfilling his penance.

Penance Sanctifies Ourselves and Others

Our penance not only makes reparation for our own sins, for it can also make reparation for the sins of others. On this, St Thomas Aquinas said:

> *as regards the payment of the debt [owed by their sins], one man can satisfy for another, provided he be in a state of charity*[9]*, so that his works may avail for satisfaction.*[10]

[8] cf. *CCC,* nos. 1474, 1477.

[9] According to St Thomas, one who is "in a state of charity" is synonymous to being in the state of grace because to have charity in the soul means to be participating in the divine nature of God: "God is love, and he who abides in him, abides in God, and God abides in him." (1 Jn 4:16).

By making sacrifices for others, we gain a greater reward for ourselves, for St Thomas also said, "He that, through charity, merits for another, at least congruously, merits more for himself."[11] Making reparation for the sins of others is not foreign to the Scriptures. For example, Moses offered himself to God as a sacrifice for the people who had sinned,[12] Job brought God a burnt offering to atone for the sins of his children,[13] and St Paul taught that we can offer sacrifices for one another.[14]

This ability to make reparation for the sins of others is possible on account of the communion of saints, because in this communion we are not only able to receive the merits of Christ's Passion directly for ourselves, we are also able, in virtue of being united to Christ, to extend those merits to others. In order to understand this particular benefit it can be helpful to know that the word, "*merit*" comes from the Greek word meaning, "*reward.*" Since our ultimate reward is the possession of God Himself – the highest good, the source of all love and perfect happiness – this notion of reward does not only refer to being united to Him in Heaven, because even here and now sanctifying grace enables us to grow in union with God on earth. Being able to merit an increase of sanctifying grace does not mean that our own charitable efforts actually produce the increase, but that God grants it to us and to others congruously as a reward. Fulton Sheen explains:

> *The communicability of merits in the communion of saints is one of the most beautiful and consoling truths taught by the Church. Love between its members does not operate only on the horizontal plane – between one person and another – but resembles a triangle; a sacrificial prayer breathed on earth is lifted up to Our High Priest, Christ in Heaven; He transubstantiates it with His merits and sends it down to earth again to enrich the sinful soul in need. As it is possible to graft skin from one part of the body to another to heal a burn, so it is possible in the Mystical Body to graft a prayer; as it is possible to transfuse blood from one healthy person*

---

[10] *Summa Theologica,* Suppl. q.13, art.2.

[11] cf. *Ibid.*

[12] cf. Ex 3:32.

[13] cf. Job 1:5.

[14] cf. Col 1:24; 2 Cor 12:15; Gal 6:2; 2 Tim 4:6.

> *to another to cure him of his weakened condition, so it is possible to transfuse sacrifice.*[15]

Since our penance helps us to sanctify not only ourselves, but others, it encourages us to see more of Christ in our brothers and sisters. It is with this awareness in mind that in 1973 the Church introduced the *Rite for Reconciliation of Several Penitents with Individual Confession and Absolution* (otherwise known as the *Second Rite*). *The Rite for Reconciliation of Individual Penitents* (otherwise known as the *First Rite)* still exists, and is the most often attended for practical reasons. Nevertheless, being a communal celebration (while retaining the essential private individual confession of sins), the Second Rite reminds us that although sin is personal it has communal repercussions. It is celebrated in due recognition of St Paul's words: "None of us lives for himself, and none of us dies to himself." "If one member suffers, all suffer together; if one member is honoured, all rejoice together. Now you are the body of Christ and individually members of it."[16] Accordingly, those who congregate to participate in the Second Rite are mindful of the opportunity they have to encourage and support one another in prayer and penance.

"Compound Interest"

All of the above benefits are compounded by the merits of Christ's Passion. Just as our money gains greater value when placed in a corporation such as a bank, so too, the merits we gain through our penitential practices are compounded to a greater degree by the infinite merits of Christ. The merits we gain thereby become far greater than they would be on their own. This analogy of a corporation such as a bank is an apt one because "*corporation*" comes from the Latin word "*corpus,*" meaning "*body.*" The Church – through which this marvellous exchange of merits takes place – is also a "corporation," namely, the *Body of Christ.* As members of Christ's Body we are able to contribute to and draw upon the "Church's treasury" of spiritual goods which consist not only of Christ's merits, but also of the prayers and good works of the Blessed Virgin Mary, of

---

[15] Fulton J Sheen, *Lift Up Your Heart* (Liguori, 1997), pp. 257-258.

[16] Rom 14:7; 1 Cor 12:26-27.

all the saints, and of all those who have by God's grace followed in the footsteps of Christ in holiness of life,[17] such that:

> *the holiness of one profits others, well beyond the harm that the sin of one could cause others. Thus recourse to the communion of saints lets the contrite sinner be more promptly and efficaciously purified of the punishments for sin.*[18]

It Builds Character

As human beings we are constituted of a *body, intellect* and *will.* Now if we can strengthen our *body* by exercise, if we can enhance our *intellect* by studying, then it is only natural that we can strengthen and perfect our *will* too through the discipline of penance. Fulton Sheen gave a good explanation as to how ascetic practices help us to grow in character. Firstly, he said many educators today forget that there is a bias toward evil in us (that is, that we are inclined to be selfish), and that unless this tendency is resisted, character suffers. Quoting Abraham Lincoln, he said, a "river always follows the line of least resistance; that is why it is crooked."

As soon as you mention "self-restraint" today, some will say: "But you should not repress yourself!" These people are unaware that when one thing is repressed, something else is liberated. If you repress evil, good comes up. If you repress good, evil comes up. If you repress the idea of telling a lie, honesty asserts itself. If a soldier represses the temptation to sleep while he is on guard, duty asserts itself. As you can see, the real question is not whether there should be repression or not – it is rather, what do you want to repress – goodness or evil?

Now that we have established that ascetic practices are good for us, let us look at the three different types of Christian discipline: Self-denial; self-restraint; and moderation. Firstly, *Self-denial:* Just as cancer has to be removed to preserve life, some evil habits cannot be overcome except by "amputating" them as it were. Being addicted to poker machines, for example, starts with a free act. The free act becomes a habit. The habit becomes a reflex, and then much of the energy that might have been used by the will to resist the habit goes into the reflex act. The result is that such a person seems to have lost power to resist the evil of excessive gambling. Should he break this evil habit with the help of God's grace

[17] cf. *CCC,* nos.1476-1477.

[18] *CCC,* no. 1475.

gradually? Or should he "amputate" them? Jesus, who knew human nature better than anyone else, recommended amputation: "If your right hand causes you to sin, cut it off and throw it away; it is better that you lose one of your members than that your whole body go into hell."[19] At this point, suppose we were considering the sin of domestic violence. Do you think a man who beats his wife should try to break this habit *gradually*, that is, to begin by beating his wife only on weekends? Of course not. If he did not "amputate" this habit he would be overlooking its serious nature, nor would he be making a decisive step to overcome his passions.

Self-restraint (otherwise known as *mortification*) is recommended when there is a mixture of good and evil. The eye is good, but it is bad for the eye to look at a light which is too bright. Just as the eye should not look at everything, so neither should the brain look at everything. Though reading is good, it is not good to put "garbage" into the brain. When the wrong kinds of images and ideas get into the mind, they seep down into the unconsciousness, and, later on, come out in evil acts. The ear is good, but it is bad for the ear if it is subjected to a sound which might break the eardrum. Likewise, it is not good to listen to backbiting, slander, evil suggestions and Godlessness. These are just a couple of examples. The same applies to all the other senses, appetites and passions.

Moderation is recommended to prevent that which is legitimately good from leading us into sin. For example, wine, ice-cream, and chocolate are all good, but consuming them could become sinful if we indulged in them to the point of gluttony or if they damaged our health.

As we can see, there are indeed benefits in *"amputating"* habits which are intrinsically evil; *restraining* habits which involve a mixture of good and evil; and *limiting* at times things which are legitimately good. We do well to consider what motivates us to practice these various forms of penance. The motivation is love. Love is not only an *affirmation*, it is also a *negation*. A man who loves a woman and asks for her hand in marriage by that very fact says no to every other woman. Likewise, a man who affirms the love of God negates the love of evil. The reason noble characters are penitential is not because they are afraid of Hell or punishment; they negate evil because they do not want to hurt the one they love.[20]

---

[19] Mt 5:30.
[20] cf. *Life is Worth Living*, pp. 97, 100-104, 253-254.

Ascetic practices not only help us with the assistance of God's grace to overcome temptation and grow in virtue, they also enable us to enjoy a greater *freedom*. Our appreciation for this freedom is understood by the awareness of our human condition: we all have freedom *of* choice, but due to sinful habits, not all of us have the freedom *to* choose. For example, a man exercises his freedom of choice by playing on poker machines, but if he is addicted to them his freedom to choose is impaired, that is, he will find it difficult to stop even if he wants to. However, if he strives to follow Christ more faithfully by practising self-denial, the more he distances himself from poker machines the more freedom he has *to* choose.

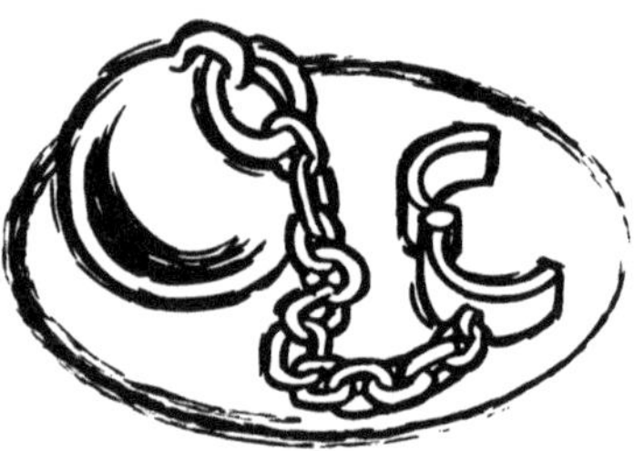

Questions for Personal Reflection or Group Discussion

Has this chapter given you a better appreciation for penance? In what way?

Does penance help you to grow in virtue and strengthen your character? Does it increase your love for Christ and His Church?

Have you ever participated in the Second Rite of Reconciliation? If so, were you encouraged by the opportunity to support and be supported by others in the common need for reconciliation, prayer and penance?

Chapter Eight

Remission of Eternal Punishment

Although many people deny the existence of Hell, it is clearly revealed in the Scriptures. There are over thirty references to Hell in the Old Testament and one-hundred-and-sixty-two references which warn of Hell in the New Testament. Over seventy of these are Christ's own words. He even told a parable specifically about Hell to convince us of its existence.[1] Jesus spoke more about Hell than all the writers of Scripture. The frequency with which He spoke about Hell has coherence with His love for us and the great Sacrifice He would make to redeem us.

Nevertheless, the following objection is often made: "How could a God of love condemn anyone to Hell?" If unrepentant sinners go to Hell it is not so much because God has condemned them to go there but more so because they have freely chosen to go there through their own rejection of God. The Church clearly states:

> *To die in mortal sin without repenting and accepting God's merciful love means remaining separated from him forever* **by our own free choice**.[2]

Unless we were deluded, we would not want to go to Hell. However, due to our human weakness we can use the gift of our free will in such a way that we choose ourselves, others, or material things over God. The gift of free choice is a precious one because it enables us to love God. But it is also a fragile gift because it enables us to offend Him by taking His love for granted, to act as if we know better than God what is good for us, and to thereby reject Him through disobedience.

Hell is not a pleasant place to contemplate in itself, especially in light

---

[1] cf. Lk 16:19-31.

[2] *CCC*, no. 1033 (Emphasis added).

of the weakness of will that we all have. Notwithstanding this, it would be foolish if the Church never reminded us of the reality of its existence, for as Pope John Paul II said, the Church cannot omit its constant catechesis on what the traditional Christian language calls the four last things of man (death, judgment, Hell and Heaven) without serious mutilation of her essential message.[3]

While it is true that a good Confession is born more from the acknowledgment of God's love for us than fear of punishment – the following reality remains the same – since the Sacrament of Reconciliation has the God-given power to remit eternal punishment it makes us appreciate God's mercy all the more.

Questions for Personal Reflection or Group Discussion

Does it surprise you that Jesus spoke on Hell more than any other subject? Why or why not?

Do you think those who are now in Heaven continue to praise God for His mercy? Why or why not?

[3] cf. *Reconciliatio et Paenitentia,* no. 26.

Chapter Nine

Temporal Punishment can be Diminished

Sin Incurs Temporal Punishment

In chapter seven we saw how sin harms the Mystical Body of Christ. Although we may have received God's forgiveness in the Sacrament of Reconciliation, if we do not make sufficient reparation for this harm in this life through our penance, then we must make up for it in Purgatory before we go to Heaven. This penance is required not only for mortal sins but for venial sins as well because they also harm Christ's Mystical Body. Unlike mortal sins, venial sins can be forgiven without sacramental confession. However, the Church recommends us to confess our venial sins[1] because while they do not extinguish sanctifying grace they still incur temporal punishment and stunt our spiritual growth.[2]

Purgatory has Coherence with God's Mercy

Although some people contest the existence of Purgatory, it is revealed in the Scriptures and is a dogmatic teaching of the Church.[3] Even though Purgatory has been traditionally described as a place where souls are purified in a "cleansing fire,"[4] this should not make us think that God is cruel. For if Purgatory did not exist, how could we truly say that God is merciful if we were condemned to Hell for all of eternity for committing some small sins or failing to do enough penance? How catastrophic would that be? If there was no place of purification we

[1] cf. *CCC,* no.1458; *Mystici Corporis Christi,* 1943, Part II; *Reconciliatio et Paenitentia,* no. 32.
[2] cf. *CCC,* no. 1863.
[3] cf. *CCC,* nos. 1030-1032.
[4] cf. *CCC,* no. 1031.

could not go to Heaven in such a state, because St John said, "nothing unclean will enter it"[5] and St Paul said, "Strive for ... that holiness without which no one will see the Lord."[6] So our Catholic belief in Purgatory does not contradict our belief in God's mercy. It is rather a marvellous affirmation of it! God has prepared a special place of purification for those who would otherwise be lost for ever. But would it not be great if we could go to Heaven without having to go to Purgatory?

Time in Purgatory can be Shortened

Now we are in a position to see that going to Confession regularly provides us with another great benefit. As human nature has it, left to our own devices we would most likely be inclined to do too little penance, for as St Ambrose said, "it is easier to find men who have kept their innocence than to find any who have done fitting penance." Although the penance we receive from the priest may not make up for *all* the reparation (otherwise known as "temporal punishment"[7]) that we owe for our sins, going to Confession often will at least give us the assurance that we will have a much shorter time in Purgatory if we need to go there at all.[8] St Thomas Aquinas said:

> *...confession diminishes the* [temporal] *punishment in virtue of the very nature of the act of the one who confesses, for this act has the punishment of shame attached to it, so that the oftener one confesses the same sins, the more is the punishment diminished. ... Consequently one who has confessed and received absolution will be less punished in Purgatory than one who has gone no further than contrition [that is, sorrow for sin].*[9]

Indulgences

In addition to the benefits we receive from the Sacrament of Penance itself, this sacrament makes it possible to receive an *indulgence*. An indulgence is a benefit that sincerely repentant Catholics can obtain that can diminish

---

5 Rev 21:27.

6 Heb12:14.

7 cf. *CCC*, no. 1472.

8 cf. *CCC*, no. 1496.

9 *SummaTheologica*, Suppl, q. 10, art.2.

the temporal punishment due to their sins as soon as possible. It can be obtained by doing works which the Church prescribes such as a prayer, a pilgrimage, or any one of many other things according to certain conditions (see *Appendix E*). In order to understand how this happens we need to see that the life of every Christian is not *individual*, but *social*. For example, I did not produce the paper these thoughts are printed on. I did not raise the cow that 'fed' me last time I ate beef. Other peoples' work allowed me to indulge in these luxuries. With this concept in mind, Fulton Sheen explains:

> *We might almost say that we are surrounded by social "indulgences," because we share in the merits, talents, arts, crafts, sciences, techniques, needlework, and genius of society.*
>
> *Now, in the society of Christ's people, His Mystical Body, it is possible to share in the merits and the good works, the prayers, the sacrifices, the self-denials, and the martyrdoms of others. If there can be an economic "indulgence," so that I can ride in a plane someone else built, why should there not also be a spiritual indulgence, so that I can be carried to Christ more quickly through the bounty of some members of the Mystical Body ...*
>
> *What a beautiful doctrine and how consoling is this sacrament! See how it combines the poor sinner who is in debt, the Mystical Body to which he is restored by absolution in the confessional, and the mercy of Christ, the Head of His Mystical Body Who gave this power to His Church: "Whatsoever thou shalt loose on earth is loosed in heaven"* [Jn 20:23].[10]

This is in keeping with how St Paul said that all the different parts of Christ's Mystical Body are to make each other's welfare their common care.[11] Here St Paul was not only writing about *social welfare*, but *spiritual welfare*. The Church declares some indulgences are even able to remit totally the temporal punishment due to sin. These are called *plenary*

[10] Archbishop Fulton Sheen, *These are the Sacraments* (New York, 1962), pp. 86-88.

[11] cf. 1 Cor 12:25.

indulgences.[12] Indulgences can even be obtained for those in Purgatory.[13] Before we are able to receive any indulgence, whether it be *partial* or *plenary,* we must have been reconciled with the Church because being in communion with Christ's Mystical Body allows us to receive this benefit. The marvellous thing about this is that just as we can harm the Church by our sins, so we can be helped by the Church when we are in debt. Fulton Sheen gives us another one of his excellent analogies to help us to see how wonderful this benefit we receive from Confession truly is:

> *...consider sin as a journey away from God. Imagine* A *is a minor son, bound to respect his father's wishes. He is in Chicago. His father,* B, *tells him to go to the left on the map – to San Francisco. But instead* A *goes to the right, to New York. When* A *gets to New York, he telephones* B *and says, "Forgive me, will you please? I am sorry for having offended you, who are deserving of my love."* B *forgives* A*; but look where* A *is! He is about nine hundred miles from his starting point, Chicago. In order to begin to do* B's *will,* A *has to go back to Chicago before he can go to San Francisco; or you could say that the nine hundred miles* A *travelled in sin must be travelled back in penance.* A *cannot begin to be good until he has retracted his evil ways.*
>
> *But like all examples, this one limps. For the fact that* A *need not walk back those 900 miles; when* A *starts, he can call upon the Church to assist him with an airplane full of the merits of our Lord, of the Blessed Mother, and the Saints. The plane flies him back the rest of the way. Such a remission in whole or in part of the punishment due to* A's *sins is effected through indulgences. Through them, the Church gives her penitents a fresh start. And the Church has a tremendous spiritual capital, gained through centuries of penance, persecution, and martyrdom; many of her children prayed, suffered, and merited more than they needed for their own individual salvation. The Church took these superabundant merits and put them into the spiritual treasury, out of which repentant sinners can draw in times of spiritual depression. Or this spiritual capital may be likened to a blood bank; whenever any of her members are suffering from*

---

[12] cf. *CCC,* no. 1471. For more information on how to gain a plenary indulgence see *Appendix E.*

[13] cf. *CCC,* nos.1479, 1498.

spiritual anaemia or the deep wounds of sin, the Church gives them a blood transfusion. She can never do it for us if we are spiritually dead in sin; a transfusion will not avail a corpse. So to obtain the indulgences or remission of the penalties of sin, the recipient must be in a state of grace, must have the intention of gaining indulgences, and must perform the prescribed works.[14]

Questions for Personal Reflection or Group Discussion

Do you see Confession as an opportunity to be free *for* holiness rather than just to be free *from* sin?

Did you know that venial sins (not just mortal sins) incur temporal punishment?

Just as you can harm Christ's Mystical Body by your sins, it comes to your aid when you are in debt. Does this increase your love for the Church?

[14] Fulton J Sheen, *Peace of Soul* (Liguori, 1996), pp. 200-201.

Chapter 10

Merits and Virtues Lost by Sin are Restored

As we have seen in chapter seven, the term "*merit*" pertains to the *reward* with which God increases His sanctifying grace within us in response to our efforts, which in turn unites us more closely to Him. The greater our union with God is on earth, the greater glory we will have in Heaven.[1] Pope Pius XI said in the Jubilee Bull, *Infinita Dei Misericordia* (1924), that to those who do penance "the fullness of the merits and the gifts which they lost through sin are restored and given back."[2] The Fathers of the Church and theologians hold this doctrine almost unanimously.[3] It has its origins in what God said through the Prophet Ezekiel:

> *But when a righteous man turns away from his righteousness and commits iniquity and does the same abominable things that the wicked man does, shall he live?* **None of the righteous deeds which he has done shall be remembered.** *(...) when a wicked man turns away from the wickedness he has committed and does what is lawful and right, he shall save his life.*[4]

Commenting on these words of the Prophet Ezekiel, St Thomas said, "Deeds done in charity are said to be deadened by a subsequent mortal sin."[5] What he goes on to say holds great promise for Confession.

He quotes what God says through the Prophet Joel: "I will restore to you the years which the swarming locust has eaten."[6] He sees the fruit that has been lost by the locusts in an allegorical sense as the "good works which were lost through sin." He concludes that meritorious deeds (deeds

---

[1] cf. Jer 17:10; Rom 2:6-7; 2 Tim 4:8; 1 Cor 3:24; Mt 5:12.

[2] *DS* 3670.

[3] cf. Dr Ludwig Ott, *Fundamentals of Catholic Dogma,* (Rockford, 1974), p. 438.

[4] Ezek 18:24,27.

[5] *Summa Theologica,* III, q. 89, art. 5.

[6] Joel 2:25.

previously performed in the state of grace) are restored and given back by Penance.[7] He even said that all the *gratuitous virtues* are restored through this sacrament.[8] (The gratuitous virtues are the seven supernatural virtues which are produced directly in the soul by God, namely, the infused *theological virtues* of faith, hope and love, and the infused *cardinal virtues* of prudence, justice, fortitude and temperance which perfect and elevate all the other virtues).

As for all the *natural virtues* such as patience, perseverance, flexibility, industriousness, etc, St Thomas said Confession does not always restore them because the effects of sin often cause them to remain weakened and diminished. This also happens on account of having a remnant of imperfect dispositions. However, sometimes God "turns the heart of man with such power, that it receives at once perfect spiritual health, not only the guilt being pardoned, but all remnants of sin being removed as was the case with Magdalene."[9]

Whether all the merits and virtues we possessed before sinning are restored, or whether these merits are increased or diminished is nothing that we can measure, but St Thomas said that they are restored in proportion to the disposition with which we receive this sacrament, so that "the penitent sometimes arises to a greater grace than that which he had before, sometimes to an equal, sometimes to a lesser; and the same applies to the virtues which flow from grace."[10] This means that the more perfect our contrition, the greater will be the measure of the merits and virtues that are restored. "*Contrition*" comes from the Latin word, "*contritio*", meaning a "*wearing down*" of that which is hardened. It is the disposition with which we try to overcome hardness of heart by the sorrow and detestation for our sins and the resolution not to sin again.

---

[7] cf. *Summa Theologica,* III, q. 89, art. 5.

[8] cf. *Ibid,* art. 1-2.

[9] *Ibid,* q. 86, art. 5.

[10] *Ibid,* q. 89, art. 2.

Questions for Personal Reflection or Group Discussion

Does this chapter resonate with your experience of making a good Confession, that is, has it helped you to grow in virtue?

Does it help to understand where the word "contrition" comes from and what it means?

Chapter Eleven

It Makes our Prayers and Good Works More Efficacious

In this chapter we will look at a number of questions that pertain to how effective a person's prayer and good works are when he is deprived of God's grace. Upon answering them we will see how the Sacrament of Reconciliation makes them more efficacious (that is, more fruitful) in virtue of the sanctifying grace that it restores within us.

Does God hear the prayers of a person in mortal sin?

First of all, if there is any question as to whether or not God hears the prayers of a person in mortal sin, St Thomas Aquinas said that God certainly does. Quoting St Augustine who was referring to the *Parable of the Pharisee and the Publican,*[1] St Thomas said, "If God were not to hear sinners, the publican would have vainly said, 'Lord, be merciful to me a sinner'."[2] A person who is not in the state of grace can pray for the grace of conversion, and when asked for with humility, confidence and perseverance, he can indeed obtain it. St Thomas said, although he cannot merit anything (because merit is a right to a reward and is thereby related to divine justice), his prayer for conversion is nevertheless heard because it is addressed to God's mercy.[3] A person's prayers for the grace of conversion would be more effective if he has the intention to go to Confession as soon as possible because it embodies the contrition necessary to receive God's grace.

[1] cf. Lk 18:9-14.
[2] *Summa Theologica,* II-II, q. 83, art. 16.
[3] cf. *Ibid.*

Can a person merit an increase of grace if he is not in the state of grace?

When a person is not in the state of grace he cannot merit an *increase* in grace by asking for it in prayer, for as St Alphonsus Liguori said, "In order to obtain God's graces by prayer, it is necessary, first, to take away sin."[4] The reason for this, as St Thomas Aquinas said, is, "Neither prayer nor any other virtuous act is meritorious without sanctifying grace."[5]

Are prayers more efficacious when sanctifying grace is in a person's soul?

St James considers that a person's prayers do indeed bear more fruit when he is reconciled to God, for he said, "the heartfelt prayer of a good man works very powerfully."[6] Since it is understood within the context of St James' words that a "good man" clearly refers to someone in the state of grace, then such a person's heartfelt prayers, provided that he is not lacking in humility,[7] are indeed more efficacious.

Does penance have any merit when a person is in mortal sin?

St Teresa said: "Nothing helps such a soul ... all the good works it might do while in mortal sin are fruitless for the attainment of glory." She explains:

> *Since these works do not proceed from that principle, which is of God ... and are separated from Him, they cannot be pleasing in His sight.*[8]

---

[4] *Sermons of St Alphonsus Liguori* (Rockford,1982), Sermon 39.
[5] *Summa Theologica,* II-II, q. 83, art. 15.
[6] Jas 5:16. (*JB*)
[7] "God opposes the proud, but gives grace to the humble." (Jas 4:6)
[8] *The Interior Castle,* I, ch. 2, no. 1.

Does the penance and good works a person offers to God while he is in mortal sin become meritorious *after* he goes to Confession?

St Thomas Aquinas said that this is not possible because without God's grace we cannot merit anything: "Works generically good done without charity are said to be dead on account of the lack of grace and charity."[9] He verifies this by quoting St Paul:

> *If I give away all I have, and if I deliver my body to be burned, but have not love, I gain nothing.*[10]

Since God *is* love,[11] St Thomas understands not having love in this context as not being in union with God. He concludes, "Therefore, it is impossible for dead works [works done in mortal sin] to be quickened [become meritorious] by Penance."[12]

In summary, there are numerous reasons to suggest that if a person has seriously neglected to go to Confession, he may be missing out on a number of benefits identified in the last two chapters because:

1 if he is in mortal sin all the penance and good works he did in the past when he was in the state of grace are "deadened," that is, they no longer have merit;

2 for as long as he is not in the state of grace (i) the penance and good works he does in that state are "dead," that is, they make no reparation for his sins, neither are they effective to win eternal life; and (ii) a good Confession does not render these dead works to have any merit;

3 the longer he is not in the state of grace, the less time and opportunity he has to gain merit for himself and others and to grow in the supernatural virtues.

However, when he makes a good Confession, the good works he did in the state of grace in the past are restored and given back. He is also able to gain graces for himself and others once more through prayer and good works, provided that he performs them with love for God and with a good intention.

---

9 *Summa Theologica,* III, q. 89, art. 6.

10 1 Cor 13:3.

11 cf. 1 Jn 4:8,16.

12 *Summa Theologica,* III, q. 89, art. 6.

Questions for Personal Reflection or Group Discussion

Does this chapter provide further reason why the frequent reception of Confession is a good practice?

Do you pray that this sacrament may be more frequently received, especially by those most in need of God's mercy?

Chapter Twelve

Priest's Prayers and Penance

In addition to our own penance, the priest is able to merit an increase of grace for ourselves through the prayers and penance he offers for us. This is why the Church says:

> *The minister of this sacrament should unite himself to the intention and charity of Christ … He must pray and do penance for his penitent, entrusting him to the Lord's mercy.*[1]

This is of particular significance because priests are called not only to participate in Christ's Priesthood by identifying themselves with Christ's holiness; they are also called to participate in Christ's Victimhood by identifying themselves with sinners. Fulton Sheen identified numerous ways that priests are called to participate in the following dimensions of Christ's Priesthood and Victimhood:

> *As a Priest, Christ was holy with the Holiness of God;*
> *as a Victim, He was "made sin."* [cf. 2 Cor 5:21]
> *As a Priest He was "separated" from the world;*
> *As a Victim He came into it to fight against the Devil, the Prince of the World.*
> *On the Cross He was upright as a Priest;*
> *On the Cross, He was prostrate as a Victim.*
> *As a priest, He mediated with the Father;*
> *As a Victim, He mediated for the sins of men.*
> *Before Pilate, He spoke seven times as the Priest-Shepherd;*
> *Before Pilate, He was silent seven times as the Victim-Lamb.*
> *As a Priest He had vertical relations with Heaven;*
> *As a Victim He had horizontal relations with earth.*
> *As a Priest He had dignity;*
> *As a Victim He suffered indignity …*

[1] *CCC*, no. 1466.

As a Priest He prays to the Father that the Cup pass;
As a Victim He drinks it to the dregs.[2]

Jesus continues to do these things in every priest, for as Fulton Sheen concluded: "If in Christ, Priesthood and Victimhood are inseparable, should this not be so in "other Christs"?"[3] To put it another way, in the priest, Christ not only intercedes for the people, He even re-lives His Passion for the sake of souls. The sacraments are of course, actions of Christ, and their effectiveness is not diminished by the imperfection or unworthiness of the priest. If the effectiveness of this sacrament is ever diminished, this is always due to the imperfect dispositions of the penitent.[4] Nevertheless, the penitent's participation in this sacrament is greatly assisted by the prayers and penance the priest offers for us due to the mysterious exchange of grace that takes place in the communion of saints.

St John Vianney longed to take on his penitents' burdens as his own, that they may not miss the glory and intimacy of God's love for which they were intended. When he said that he was afraid of discouraging his penitents if he were to impose severe penances, a brother priest responded, "But how can we strike a happy middle course in this matter?" "My friend," the saint replied, "here is my receipt: I give them a small penance and the remainder I myself perform in their stead."[5] In a sense, he wanted to compel God to grant many graces to his penitents not only by his ardent prayers but by the many sacrifices he was known to make for them. He never ceases to be an example, ever living, ever relevant, to many confessors. Given that priests are called to model their lives on this great exemplar of the confessional, there is no reason for penitents to feel belittled by the sacrifices confessors make

---

[2] Fulton J Sheen, *Those Mysterious Priests* (New York, 1974), p. 30.

[3] *Ibid,* p.32.

[4] St Thomas Aquinas said: "*Penance, considered in itself, has the power to bring all defects back to perfection, and even to advance man to a higher state; but this is sometimes hindered on the part of man, whose movement towards God and in detestation of sin is too remiss.*" *Summa Theologica,* III, q. 89, art. 3.

[5] Abbé Francis Trochu, *The Curé D' Ars – St Jean-Marie-Baptiste Vianney,* trans. Dom Ernest Graf, OSB (Rockford,1977), p. 297.

for them because let us not forget that priests need to make sacrifices for their own sins![6] Speaking for myself, whenever penitents become emotional in their sorrow and/or ask me to pray for them, it moves me to want to offer sacrifices for them because I can relate to their desire to make reparation for their sins. If more people came to Confession, imagine how much more priests themselves would grow in holiness.

This is not to say that priests do not need the prayers and sacrifices of the laity. St Paul openly acknowledged his personal struggle with sin[7] and requested the people's prayers on his behalf.[8] Although the laity are not part of the *Ministerial Priesthood*, they are, nevertheless, part of the *Royal Priesthood* on account of being members of Christ's Mystical Body through the Sacrament of Baptism. This means that their prayers and sacrifices are efficacious too. Were they not, St Peter's exhortation would have made no sense when he said to the lay faithful, "Like living stones, let yourselves be built into a spiritual house, to be a holy priesthood, to offer spiritual sacrifices acceptable to God through Jesus Christ."[9]

So, inasmuch as priests are called to pray and make sacrifices for the people they serve, do not forget that they need your prayers and sacrifices too. This understanding enables both priests and the laity to feel responsible toward one another as the various parts of the human body do, for as St Paul said, "The eye cannot say to the hand, 'I have no need of you,' nor again the head to the feet, 'I have no need of you'."[10]

Questions for Personal Reflection or Group Discussion

Is it encouraging to know that priests are called to pray and do penance for penitents?

Do you pray and make spiritual sacrifices for your priests?

---

[6] cf. Heb 7:27.
[7] cf. Rom 7:15-24.
[8] cf. Eph 6:19-20; Col 4:4; 2 Thess 3:2; Heb 13:18-19.
[9] 1 Pet 2:5.
[10] 1 Cor 12:21.

Chapter Thirteen

More Fruitful Participation in the Other Sacraments

We have seen that one of the benefits of Confession is that it confers sanctifying grace and sacramental grace. Perhaps you already know that the other sacraments we receive after baptism also provide these graces according to the purpose for which each of these sacraments is given. However, what many people do not realise is that the Church teaches that no one can receive these graces from the Sacraments of the Eucharist, Confirmation, Marriage, and Holy Orders if they are not in the state of grace.[1] The parable of the *Vine and the Branches*[2] helps us to understand this. If we (the branches) separate ourselves from the vine (Christ), then how could we expect the sacraments to "bear fruit"[3] in us given that we are no longer receiving the sap? (God's grace is like the sap which makes the sacraments efficacious.) Just as Jesus said, "As the branch cannot bear fruit by itself, unless it abides in the vine, neither can you, unless you abide in me … for apart from me you can do nothing,"[4] neither can the other sacraments do anything if, through sin, we do not abide in Christ and He in us.

In practical terms this means that if we are not in the state of grace when we receive the Sacraments of the Eucharist, Confirmation,

[1] cf. Dr Ludwig Ott, in *Fundamentals of Catholic Dogma,* p. 346.
[2] cf. Jn 14:4-8.
[3] cf. Jn 15:4.
[4] Jn 15:4-5.

Marriage, and Holy Orders (known as the *Sacraments of the Living*[5]), these sacraments are validly received but we receive no graces from them. Or, if we had received these sacraments worthily, but had subsequently committed a mortal sin, we would not continue to receive the graces from these sacraments. It is comforting to know then that the Church teaches:

> *The Sacraments of Baptism, Confirmation and Consecration* [Marriage and Holy Orders], *when they are received validly but unworthily, revive after the removal of the moral indisposition, that is, the sacramental grace is conferred subsequently.*[6]

It is clear then that if we have committed a serious sin we need to go to Confession if we wish to benefit from these other sacraments. The Sacrament of Reconciliation is necessary in this sense because the Church teaches:

> *Individual and integral confession of grave sins followed by absolution remains the only ordinary means of reconciliation with God and with the Church.*[7]

Let us have a look then at the particular graces given by these sacraments that revive within us after we go to Confession. So doing, this will help us to see the numerous benefits that this sacrament indirectly provides.

Sacrament of the Eucharist

Our participation in the Eucharist (i) delivers us from venial sins; (ii) preserves, increases, and renews sanctifying grace received at Baptism; (iii) increases union with Christ; (iv) renews, strengthens, and deepens our incorporation into the Church, already

[5] These sacraments are called the *Sacraments of the Living* because those who receive them fruitfully are already in the state of grace. The *Sacraments of the Dead* are the sacraments which confer sanctifying grace for the first time (Baptism), or sanctifying grace which has been lost (Sacrament of Reconciliation).

[6] Dr Ludwig Ott, *Fundamentals of Catholic Dogma,* p. 346.

[7] *CCC,* no. 1497.

achieved by Baptism; (v) helps to preserve us from future mortal sins; and (vi) strengthens the spiritual life.[8]

If we were not in the state of grace we would not derive any of these benefits above from receiving Holy Communion. Some people argue that receiving the Eucharist before confessing serious sins can be justified on the grounds that the Eucharist provides them with Christ's strength to overcome temptation. However, let us not forget three important things that we need to bear in mind: (i) no such strength is derived from receiving Holy Communion when a person knowingly receives Our Lord unworthily; (ii) strength to overcome temptation is not unique to the Eucharist, for as we have seen, the Sacrament of Reconciliation itself also provides us with the graces we need to struggle against temptation and to even grow in virtue; and more importantly (iii) since we are not only receiving grace from the Eucharist but the *Author* of grace Himself, Jesus Christ, who is truly present under the appearance of bread and wine, surely we would want to be properly disposed to receive Him. For these reasons the Church clearly teaches:

> *The Eucharist is not ordered to the forgiveness of mortal sins – that is proper to the sacrament of Reconciliation. The Eucharist is properly the sacrament of those who are in full communion with the Church.*[9]

For the same reason, the Church also clearly teaches:

> *Anyone who is aware of having committed a mortal sin must not receive Holy Communion, even if he experiences deep contrition, without having first received sacramental absolution, unless he has a grave reason for receiving Communion and there is no possibility of going to confession.*[10]

We need to be reminded of this because as Pope John Paul II said:

> *There are serious reasons for astonishment and anxiety when one sees, in certain areas, so many of the faithful receiving the Eucharist when such a small number of them has recourse to the sacrament of reconciliation.*[11]

---

[8] cf. *CCC,* nos. 1391-1396.

[9] *CCC,* no. 1395.

[10] *CCC,* no. 1457; *CIC,* can. 916; *Reconciliatio et Paenitentia,* no. 27.

[11] Address to French bishops, 2 April 1982.

Pope Benedict XVI also acknowledged this as he states:

> *the faithful are surrounded by a culture that tends to eliminate the sense of sin and to promote a superficial approach that overlooks the need to be in a state of grace in order to approach sacramental communion worthily.*[12]

Catholics would be further convinced of the Church's teaching about being properly disposed to receive Holy Communion if they all knew of St Paul's strong admonition. He said that anyone who "eats the bread or drinks the cup of the Lord in an unworthy manner will be guilty of profaning the body and blood of the Lord."[13] What he means by an "unworthy manner" is clear from what he immediately goes on to say:

> *Let a man examine himself, and so eat of the bread and drink of the cup. For any one who eats and drinks without discerning the body eats and drinks judgment upon himself.*[14]

While what he says here applies first and foremost to belief in the Real Presence in the Eucharist, this belief has moral implications, for as Pope John Paul II said:

> *"To discern the Body of the Lord" means, in the doctrine of the Church, to dispose oneself to receive the Eucharist with purity of soul which, in the case of grave sin, requires the previous reception of the Sacrament of Penance.*[15]

So, from our understanding of what St Paul said, receiving Holy Communion when we are conscious of serious sin profanes the Eucharist in the most grievous manner. It adds a new sin to those of which we were already guilty. Thus, to protect the Blessed Sacrament from being improperly received Pope John II reminded us of St John Chrysostom's warning:

> *I too raise my voice, I beseech, beg and implore that no one draw near to this sacred table with a sullied and corrupt conscience. Such an act, in fact, can never be called 'communion', not even*

[12] Post-Synodal Apostolic Exhortation, *On the Eucharist as the Source and Summit of the Church's Life and Mission (Sacramentum Caritatis)*, 2007, no. 20.

[13] 1 Cor 11:27.

[14] 1 Cor 11:28-29.

[15] General Audience, 18 April 1984.

> *were we to touch the Lord's body a thousand times over, but 'condemnation', 'torment' and 'increase of punishment'.*[16]

Pope Benedict XVI stated that the relationship between the Eucharist and the Sacrament of Reconciliation "reminds us that sin is never a purely individual affair; it always damages the ecclesial communion that we have entered through Baptism" and that Reconciliation emphasises "that the outcome of the process of conversion is also the restoration of full ecclesial communion, expressed in a return to the Eucharist."[17]

While the Penitential Rite at the beginning of Mass prepares us to participate in the Sacred Mysteries we celebrate, the Church teaches that unlike the Sacrament of Reconciliation, it cannot provide remission for serious sins.[18] As for venial sins, these do not make us unworthy to receive Holy Communion because we can receive God's forgiveness for them during our participation in the Mass. However, an attachment to venial sins does prevent us from receiving the more abundant graces which we would otherwise receive. Therefore, the more often we go to Confession, the more conscious will be our efforts to be as perfectly disposed as we can be to derive greater fruits from the Eucharist. This does not mean that we should go to Confession *every* time before we go to Mass if we have no serious sins to confess. While the Church is trying to address the lack of reverence for the Eucharist that has become commonplace on one hand, she does not want to lead people to be too rigorous or scrupulous on the other.

Sacrament of Confirmation

The Sacrament of Confirmation not only intensifies and increases the life of God within us by communicating to our soul sanctifying grace, it also (i) gives us sacramental graces that provide us with supernatural strength and courage to profess and live our faith with

[16] *The Eucharist and the Church (Ecclesia de Eucharistia),* 2003, no. 36.

[17] *Sacramentum Caritatis*, no. 20.

[18] cf. Congregation for Divine Worship and the Sacraments, *Certain Matters to be Observed or to be Avoided regarding the Most Holy Eucharist (Redemptionis Sacramentum),* 2004, no. 80.

constancy and to never to be ashamed of the Cross; (ii) it unites us more firmly to Christ and renders our bond with the Church more perfect; and (iii) the Holy Spirit dwells within us, bringing to our soul the abundance of His divine gifts.[19] These *gifts of the Holy Spirit* include: wisdom, understanding, knowledge, right judgment, courage, reverence, and wonder which are infused supernatural dispositions to help us act in accordance with the inspirations and motions of the Holy Spirit. In turn, these sevenfold gifts of the Holy Spirit perfect the seven *supernatural virtues* because each of these gifts correspond with them. (The supernatural virtues consist of the *theological virtues* of faith, hope and love, and the *cardinal virtues* of prudence, justice, temperance, and fortitude.) By these virtues, we are aided to withstand the obstacles and opposition we may meet in the practice of the faith and in our own spiritual progress. The graces we receive from this sacrament also enable us to make Christ more attractive and appealing to others.

Sacrament of Marriage

The Church teaches that the grace proper to the Sacrament of Marriage is given to: (i) perfect the couple's love and to strengthen their indissoluble unity; (ii) to help one another to attain holiness in their married life; and (iii) welcome and educate their children.[20] In practice, receiving these graces means:

> *Christ dwells with them, gives them strength to take up their crosses and so follow him, to rise again after they have fallen, to forgive one another, to bear one another's burdens, to "be subject to one another out of reverence for Christ" [Eph 5:21; cf. Gal 6:2] and to love one another with supernatural, tender, and fruitful love. In the joys of their love and family life he gives them here on earth a foretaste of the wedding feast of the Lamb.*[21]

---

[19] cf. *CCC,* no. 1303.

[20] cf. *CCC,* no. 1641.

[21] *CCC,* no. 1642.

These graces are indeed of great assistance, but as long as spouses remain unreconciled to God who is the giver of these graces and the source of love itself, they are unable to receive the benefit of this beautiful sacrament. Knowing this, there is reason to believe that today's divorce rates would not be so high if more Catholic couples availed themselves of the Sacrament of Reconciliation.

Sacrament of Holy Orders

Even if an ordained minister is not in the state of grace, the sacraments that he administers are always valid and confer grace on those who receive them. However, he would not be able to receive the sacramental graces that Holy Orders provide to help him in his own spiritual life. These graces help him, whether he is a deacon, priest, or bishop to perform his duties in a spirit of holiness. Such assistance further complements and develops his growth in grace and charity demanded by the supreme commandment.[22]

While the Sacrament of Holy Orders gives a priest the power to act in the Person of Christ, God would never confer this power on any man without giving him, at the same time, the grace he needs to exercise that power worthily. This is why, according to St Thomas Aquinas, it

[22] cf. *DS* 960. The supreme commandment is to love God with all our heart, soul and mind and to love our neighbour as ourself. cf. Mt 22:37-39).

[23] cf. *Summa Theologica,* I-II, q. 62, Introduction.

follows that this grace provides even more precious an effect than the power to act in Christ's name itself.[23]

Questions for Personal Reflection or Group Discussion

Can you see why the recommended practice of going to Confession before receiving any other sacrament after Baptism is praiseworthy?

Do you think the world would be a better place if Catholics went to Confession more frequently?

Chapter Fourteen

Sacrament of Healing

Every sin affects us in three ways. Depending upon the degree of its gravity, it: (i) disrupts or estranges our relationship with God; (ii) disturbs or alienates our relationship with our neighbours; and (iii) unsettles us internally or makes us suffer from self-estrangement. These effects make us aware of our need for healing, especially when internal turmoil results from the struggle for self-mastery. St Paul articulated this well:

> *I do not understand my own actions. For I do not do what I want, but I do the very thing I hate ... So then it is no longer I that do it, but sin which dwells within me ... I can will what is right, but I cannot do it. For I do not do the good I want, but the evil I do not want is what I do ... I delight in the law of God, in my inmost self, but I see in my members another law at war with the law of my mind and making me captive to the law of sin which dwells in my members.*[1]

Here reason dictates that just as our bodies become physically sick when suffering from a disease, our souls also become "sick" whenever we suffer the consequences of sin. Perhaps this "sickness" can be best described in terms of an *imbalance* and *emptiness*. Let us look at sin firstly in terms of an *imbalance* and how Confession helps to restore balance. Tradition tells us that when Adam and Eve sinned (known as *original sin*) human nature became

[1] Rom 7:15,17-19,22-23.

wounded. This fallen state, this weakness in our human nature is called "concupiscence." As a result of original sin our intellect, will, and appetites can become misdirected away from our *ultimate end* (God is our ultimate end because being united to Him in love in eternal happiness is the ultimate purpose for which He made us) to mere *proximate ends* (things for which we were not made). As a consequence of original sin and our own personal sins, our ability to *reason*, *choose* and *desire* become less inclined to virtue:

- when our appetites become disordered they have a tendency to pull our intellect down into darkness such that our minds fail to behold the truth[2];
- our will becomes misdirected, not to God as our ultimate end but to creatures as proximate ends; and
- our appetites become disordered such that our desire for food, sleep, and sexual intimacy no longer become ordered to a virtuous end as they were created to be but to ourselves. Our appetites thereby have a tendency to drag us down into gluttony, laziness, lust, and other habitual sins.

The more we sin, the less we are inclined to virtue. Sin thereby wounds our human nature. This is why the Church calls Confession a "sacrament of healing."[3] It provides us with the graces we need that bring healing to these wounds such that our intellect, will and appetites become more inclined to virtue. As a result, we are endowed with greater freedom to do what is good.

There is another way in which the "sickness" of sin can be spoken of as an imbalance. Whenever we give in to temptation, we do so because we are looking for goodness, truth and love – things that we expect to make us feel happy – but we use a disordered means to obtain them. For example, a man might rob a bank to have a comfortable life. There is nothing wrong with wanting comfort, but he has used a disordered means to attain it. Moreover, he has exchanged an earthly good (a proximate end) for Christ (our ultimate end). St Alphonsus Liguori

---

[2] cf. Wis 9:15.

[3] *CCC,* no. 1421

explains how this imbalance is a gross injustice towards the infinite goodness of God:

> *God is an infinite good; and when he sees sinners put him on a level with some earthly trifle or with a miserable gratification, he justly complains in the language of the prophet: "To whom have you likened me or made me equal?* [Is 46:5] *In your estimation, a vile pleasure is more valuable than my grace. Is it a momentary satisfaction you have preferred before me? "Thou hast cast me off behind thy back"* [Ezek 23:35].[4]

This is strong language for modern readers, but his words have merit because they highlight the way sin undermines our spiritual health. Just as clinical depression is diagnosed as a sickness due to a chemical imbalance in the brain, so too, sin is rightly called a "sickness" due to a spiritual imbalance in our soul, an imbalance that is brought about by our disordered desires. What is so bad about this imbalance? What or who determines the equilibrium? Christ. This imbalance is not good because it means that Christ – the true source of our eternal happiness, He who is Love, Goodness and Truth itself – is no longer the centre of our lives; He no longer dwells in the centre of our soul, and even though we may not be conscious of that reality, this imbalance is nevertheless registered deeply within us, for as St Augustine said, "You [God] have made us for yourself, and our hearts find no peace until they rest in you."[5]

This imbalance is further exacerbated by the experience of feeling tremendously *empty* inside. Pride deceived us into thinking that we had found something that would fulfil our desires for love, goodness and truth only to discover that we have fallen for a counterfeit. This leaves us feeling emptier inside than we were before. For those who have fallen into serious sin, a vicious circle can quickly ensue within them, because in their desperation to fill that deep void they can very easily keep falling into the same sin again and again.

St John of the Cross provides an insight as to why we feel this emptiness. He says that the capacity of the human soul is deep because our hearts are made for God. Since God is infinite, in a sense the capacity of our

---

[4] Sermon 6.

[5] St Augustine, *Confessions*, Bk. 1, art. 1.

soul to accommodate Him must also be infinite. This is why our thirst and hunger for love is deep and in a certain fashion infinite.[6] This being the case, when we try to fill the emptiness within ourselves with things that are only finite we feel even emptier inside. Hence our unhappiness and anxieties, our disappointments and our sadness. St John of the Cross makes the conclusion that since the emptiness of our soul is a living reflection of God who is infinite, our desire for love cannot find fulfilment in anything other than God.[7]

Knowing this increases our appreciation for the wonderful healing effects the Sacrament of Reconciliation has upon us. Whenever we acknowledge in Confession that we have given in to any inordinate desires that cause this interior imbalance and emptiness, we are giving Christ the opportunity to help us centre our desires more on Him. Moreover, by doing this, Christ is able to fill us with the greatest of all His gifts – *Himself.* In so doing, the indwelling Trinity (Father, Son and Holy Spirit) ends up in a much deeper and more central place in our hearts: "If a man loves me, he will keep my word, and my Father will love him, and we will come to him and make our home with him."[8]

This is why it is so important that our sense of guilt always be in relation to Christ and His mercy because without Christ we have no one to heal the wounds caused by our sins. In other words, the *misery* of our guilt and the *mercy* of Christ must always go together: misery without mercy leads to despair, mercy without misery leads to the arrogant presumption that God will forgive us, however, misery *with* mercy leads to contrition which makes reconciliation with God and its healing effects possible.

Although Judas Iscariot "repented"[9] he did not turn to Christ. Rather, he only turned inwards to himself. In his guilt he did not look for Christ's mercy and so he ended up in despair. If in the misery of his guilt Judas turned to Christ he would have encountered His healing mercy. This is why Pope John Paul II describes how we are able to experience "a healing of a medicinal character"[10] in Confession because it enables us to

---

[6] cf. *The Living Flame of Love,* stanza 3, no. 22.
[7] cf. *Ibid.*
[8] Jn 14:23.
[9] Mt 27:3.
[10] *Reconciliatio et Paenitentia,* no. 31.

encounter Christ's compassionate and merciful love. Quoting St Augustine, Pope John Paul II said, "It is thanks to the medicine of confession that the experience of sin does not denigrate into despair."[11]

Once we have gone to Confession, further healing can take place through our penance, for as St John Chrysostom said:

> *It is not enough to remove the arrow from the body. We also have to heal the wound caused by the arrow. It is the same with the soul; after we have received forgiveness for our sins, we have to heal the wound that remains through penance.*[12]

A good Confessor will give us penance that is 'customised' to directly oppose and counteract the sinful habit we have confessed. In addition to strengthening our character, performing a well prescribed penance can bring further healing to the wounds caused by our sins.

Questions for Personal Reflection or Group Discussion

Does your own experience of needing God's mercy correspond with a certain sense of imbalance and emptiness?

What do you think of St John of the Cross' words on how the human soul's capacity to accommodate God is, in a certain sense, infinite?

Have you become aware of the healing effects of the Sacrament of Reconciliation in your life?

[11] *Ibid.*

[12] Homily on the Gospel of St Matthew, no. 3, 5.

Chapter Fifteen

It Strengthens our Faith

St Alphonsus Liguori said, "Every sin produces darkness in the understanding. Hence, the more sins are multiplied by a bad habit, the greater the blindness they cause."[1] This happens because our moral life is not separate from our intellectual life. We are less inclined to be convinced by the truth if we are not living it, because the way we live has an influence on the way we think. Fulton Sheen explains this well:

> *Pour water into the red glass and it looks red; pour it into a green glass and it looks green; pour it into a black glass and it will look black. When you pour truth into mind* A *and pour it into mind* B, *it does not have the same effect, though it is identically the same truth.* A *may accept it, and* B *does not. The difference is not in the truth; rather the difference is in the mental soil in which the seed of truth is planted. It is not ignorance alone that is the cause of unbelief. Another and more important cause is behaviour … A French infidel once said to Pascal, "If I had your principles, I would be a better man." Pascal said, "Begin with being a better man, and you will soon have my principles." If we do not live as we think, we soon begin to think as we live; we make a philosophy to suit our bad behaviour … men often question truth because they hate it in practice. If they changed their lives they would change their thinking. Scepticism is not an intellectual position but a moral position.*[2]

It is easy to find truth. It can be hard to face it, and harder still to follow it on account of how our faith affects us personally. This cannot be said of any other science because unlike the truths of our Faith, the truths of science are abstract, impersonal and a-ethical. For example, a man's moral

[1] Sermon 20.

[2] Fulton Sheen, *Life is Worth Living* (San Francisco,1999), p. 254.

behaviour is unlikely to be improved when he learns about the principles of geometry because it does not affect him personally. Whereas if a man who is given over to sensuality and promiscuity encounters the Person of Christ and His teachings on purity and chastity, it is only natural that he will want to resist these teachings because they threaten the bad habits he has come to love as portions of himself. Furthermore, his sins can prevent God's grace from coming in because they become like dirt on a window impeding the sunlight. Consequently he can feel confused by the Christian Faith. If any of the light of God's truth does get through, he wards it off and bars it out, because his will is bent on his inordinate desires. His will does not allow him to admit the truth presented to his mind. This is just one example.

St John identified the three kinds of 'dirt' that can accumulate as bad habits on the 'window' of the soul that keep God's grace from coming in. These are 'carnal dirt' (inordinate love of fleshly pleasures); 'money dirt' (the lust of material things); and 'ego-centric dirt', (pride, selfishness and vanity).[3] Given that St John said that these desires are "not of the Father" but "of the world"[4] it is only natural that when a person gives in to such desires they condition him to have a vision for only worldly, finite and temporal things. Thereby his ability to see things which lead him to the divine, infinite and eternal are diminished. Consequently, anything which is of God, faith, or religion does not make sense, or at least he can be confused by these things, because they are beyond his field of vision. Even if such things were visible to him, they would seem distasteful, as his will has become accustomed to enjoy sinful pleasures.

These examples could be considered extreme and we may not be able to relate to them immediately, but if we allow ourselves to grow accustomed to any kind of sin – however small – it can cloud the window of our soul, impeding our ability to grow in faith. This is why Jesus said:

[3] cf. 1 Jn 2:16.

[4] *Ibid.*

> *...though the light has come into the world men have shown they prefer darkness to the light because their deeds were evil. And indeed, everybody who does wrong hates the light and avoids it.*[5]

Jesus was particularly mindful of this principle when He spoke to those whose lifestyle was contrary to the Gospel. So He reminded them what the Prophet Isaiah had said:

> *You shall indeed hear but never understand, and you shall indeed see but never perceive. For this people's heart has grown dull, and their ears are heavy of hearing, and their eyes they have closed, lest they should perceive with their eyes, and hear with their ears, and understand with their heart, and turn for me to heal them.*[6]

To those who were trying to be faithful to His teachings, however, Jesus said, "Happy are your eyes because they see, your ears because they hear!"[7] It follows, therefore, that when we make a good Confession, when we repent and try to live the Gospel with growing fidelity, our faith makes greater sense and it gives us greater conviction. This particular benefit of Confession would especially be true for those who have denied their faith or who have ceased to practise it.

According to the *Parable of the Sower,*[8] the more faithful we are to the Gospel, the more God endows us with the gift of faith. The seed signifies the gift of faith which grows abundant fruit when it is planted in rich soil, and the rich soil signifies those who not only listen to Christ's teachings but try to live them.

Christ further clarified how faith is increased in us according to this parable when He said, "For to him who has, more will be given, and he will have abundance; but from him who has not, even what he has will be taken away."[9] While the Sacrament of Penance can increase and strengthen our faith when we have recourse to it, much of our faith could "be taken away"[10] without it. This could happen on account of not having such a good means by which we can pursue the ongoing conversion that is necessary to keep our minds "in tune" with God's

[5] Jn 3:20. (*JB*)
[6] Mt 13:14-15.
[7] Mt 13:16.
[8] cf. Mt 13:3-43.
[9] Mt 13:12.
[10] cf. *Ibid.*

"wavelength." It encourages us to be honest with ourselves so that we can recognise the desires, attitudes and habits we have that impede our capacity to embrace and act upon the Faith we profess. Jesus went so far as to thank His Father for hiding the truth from those whose intelligence was corrupted by arrogance and revealing it to the little ones[11] because he knew that they would live by this truth. By returning us to the simplicity and innocence of little children, the Sacrament of Penance thereby enables us to understand better the truths of our Faith. Fulton Sheen illustrated this understanding by relating the following conversion experience of an atheist:

> *A young woman wrote to me – she was a college student – she said, "I've given up my faith. I no longer believe in God, and I am now an atheist."*
>
> *Well I was curious, that she should have first of all written to me. She lived in another city. I wrote to her and asked her to call on me … I said, "How did you happen to lose your faith?" (In other words, I was asking her, "What was the 'scapegoat?' What's the excuse?") She said, "My studies in comparative religion: I was part of a class and found out all religions are alike."*
>
> *Well sure, all the paintings in the gallery have the same colour, but that doesn't mean that they were painted by the same artist. But at any rate, that was the reason she gave. I knew of course, that was not the real reason. But I played along with it for a minute. And she was in my library, and I said, "Now, directly behind you is a section of books on comparative religion. I have about four-hundred different titles on that subject. Now, you pick out any of those books you know and we will discuss it. Now, glance them over." She didn't know any of them which didn't a bit surprise me. I said, "My good girl, come into Confession." She said, "How can I go to Confession? I don't even believe in God!" I said, "Now listen. You're not having any difficulty with the Creed. You have difficulties with the Commandments. Why don't you face up to it? You've been immoral. In order to escape your sense of guilt, you wrote to me about being an atheist. Isn't that right?" She said, "Yes, that's right." Well, she went to Confession. She was alright!* [her faith returned].[12]

[11] cf. Mt 11:25; Lk 10:21.

[12] Fulton J Sheen, *Life is Worth Living*, vol. 5, "Guilt" (Soundtrack of TV Broadcast).

Questions for Personal Reflection or Group Discussion

Does your own experience correspond with Fulton Sheen's axiom: "If we do not live as we think, we soon begin to think as we live"?

Have you ever noticed that your faith has become strengthened after making a good Confession?

Do you recommend those you know who have become lax in their faith to go to Confession? If they are anxious, do you recommend them to see those who are known to be good Confessors? Do you know where the priests are in your local area who are known for their compassion and ability to give good guidance?

Chapter Sixteen

It Cultivates Hope

Some people do not come to Confession because they know that there are certain sins that they keep falling into, sins that they think they will never be able to overcome due to the overwhelming nature of the temptations that lead to them. This is especially true of sins that are addictive, such as drug and alcohol abuse, gambling, overeating and unchastity, and sins which involve passion, such as anger and lust. Since they do not believe they have the strength to overcome such temptations, they become terribly disheartened and afraid that they will fall into the same sin again, and so they can often think, "Why bother going to Confession? I'm going to fall again anyway!" The Church is well aware of why such an enslavement to sin can take place:

> *Sin creates a proclivity to sin; it engenders vice by repetition of the same acts. This results in perverse inclinations which cloud conscience and corrupt the concrete judgment of good and evil. Thus sin tends to reproduce itself and reinforce itself.*[1]

Those who do not have the heart to go to Confession due to being caught up in addictive sins can end up being torn up inside. While they suffer from the attachment to sin on one hand, they also suffer from the wounds of their sins on the other, which serves as a constant reminder of their need for God's love, mercy, and healing. Their "Why bother" attitude (that is, their belief that they are unable to change) comes from the acknowledgment that human effort alone is insufficient. However, they err by overlooking that it is precisely because human effort alone is insufficient (especially when addictive habits and/or passions are involved) that we need God's grace.

---

[1] *CCC,* no. 1865.

St John Vianney said, "The reason why we cannot keep our good resolutions is that we count too much on *ourselves*."[2] What often prevents penitents from seeking God's grace in Confession can be their desire to avoid the shame associated with having to go back to confess the same sin again. A person once told a priest, "I've been trying to overcome this temptation by myself for years. I didn't want to come to Confession until I thought I was on top of it." This kind of thinking is unfortunate because it overlooks how the Sacrament of Reconciliation cultivates hope.

Knowing that the Sacrament of Reconciliation is an avenue of God's grace enables us to appreciate it as a formidable means by which we can overcome our weaknesses. Furthermore, relying on God in this way thereby helps us to see that there is no such thing as a hopeless situation. Hope is indeed cultivated because the graces we are able to receive from this sacrament can help us to achieve what is otherwise humanly impossible, for as St Paul said, "the power at work within us is able to do far more abundantly than all that we ask or think."[3]

St Paul said something else which is also consistent with our understanding of the Sacraments: "God is at work in you, both to *will* and to *work* for his good pleasure."[4] Our *will* to repent and change our ways, and our desire to *work* for our salvation are aided by the graces we receive in this sacrament. The Church teaches that if we do not place an obstacle to the sacraments, they produce grace by themselves "by the very fact of the actions being performed."[5] In other words, the sacraments produce grace from the fact that Christ gave them to His Church so that He could apply His merits to us through her. Just as St Luke said in his Gospel, that power came forth from Christ that healed and transformed those who came into contact with His body,[6] this same power, through the activity of the Holy Spirit, continues to come forth from Christ's

[2] *Thoughts of the Curé D'Ars,* compiled & arranged by W.M.B (Rockford, 1984), p. 9.
[3] Eph 3:20.
[4] Phil 2:13.
[5] *CCC,* no. 1128.
[6] cf. Lk 5:17; 6:19; 8:46.

Mystical Body, the Church. St Paul qualifies this further when he said that the Church's power is the same as the mighty strength God used when He raised Christ from death.[7]

When received worthily in faith, the sacraments confer the grace that they signify. They are *efficacious* (that is, they produce their desired effect) because in them Christ Himself is at work. It is He who acts in the sacraments.[8] This is why the Church calls the sacraments the "masterworks of God"![9]

It may take some time to overcome addictive vices and sins that involve passion because bad habits cannot always be overcome overnight. It can be embarrassing to have to confess the same sins. However, over time such efforts are worth it because progress is nevertheless made when human perseverance is aided by the grace of God attained through prayer and the frequent reception of this sacrament.

Further reasons as to why it takes time to overcome sins we struggle with can be seen when we consider that the graces we receive in this sacrament fall on our *soul*, not on our *body*. For example, a person who has a habit of drinking excessively cannot expect his tastebuds to be altered by a sincere confession. His taste for alcohol remains. Nevertheless, for those who confess their sins with perfect contrition and a firm desire not to sin again, it is not uncommon for them to feel a huge strength which remains with them unless they put themselves into another occasion of sin voluntarily. This experience of strength happens on account of the Sacrament of Reconciliation, for as we have seen in chapters five and ten, God restores and/or increases the graces and virtues we need when we confess our sins with good dispositions. This also disposes us to receive further increase of grace in our participation in the Mass and reception of Holy Communion. Since Jesus is able to do so much in the souls of those who go to Confession, He told St Faustina that this sacrament brings about the greatest miracles:

> *Write, speak of My mercy. Tell souls where they are to look for solace; that is, in the Tribunal of Mercy [the Sacrament of Reconciliation]. There the greatest miracles take place [and] are*

[7] cf. Eph 1:19.
[8] cf. *CCC*, no. 1128.
[9] *CCC*, no. 1116.

incessantly repeated. To avail oneself of this miracle, it is not necessary to go on a great pilgrimage or to carry out some external ceremony; it suffices to come with faith to the feet of My representative and to reveal to him one's misery, and the miracle of Divine Mercy will be fully demonstrated. Were a soul like a decaying corpse so that from a human standpoint, there would be no [hope of] restoration and everything would already be lost, it is not so with God. The miracle of Divine Mercy restores that soul in full. Oh, how miserable are those who do not take advantage of the miracle of God's mercy! You will call out in vain but it will be too late.[10]

Questions for Personal Reflection or Group Discussion

Do you agree with St John of the Cross who said, "The soul obtains from God as much as it hopes for"?

St Teresa of Avila said that if we pray and sin, only two things can happen: we can keep sinning and stop praying, or keep praying and stop sinning. Does this correlate with your experience?

Has the Sacrament of Reconciliation made you more confident in God's grace?

[10] *Divine Mercy in my Soul: Diary of Sister M. Faustina Kowalska*, no. 1448.

Chapter Seventeen

It Increases Charity

The Church teaches that mortal sin results in the *loss of charity*. This happens on account of how it turns our back against God, cutting us off from the source of love itself. Mortal sin is thereby incompatible with the virtue of charity, the vital principle within us which comes from God and unites us to Him.[1] This does not mean that this kind of sin prevents us from having any capacity to love at all. Nevertheless, it does incline the virtue of charity to become distorted, such that we begin to love others only for our own sake. Such selfishness differs greatly from authentic love which has as its object the goodness of God and others whom we love for His sake. Authentic charity also enables us to love ourselves for God's sake. This is not to be confused with vanity; rather it is a healthy sense of self-worth which arises from the acknowledgement that we are loved by God. This does much to dispel self-hatred, disappointment and shame that can often emerge in consequence of sin.

When the theological virtue of charity is given back to us in Confession, it is not just a simple matter of having an important virtue restored, for as this takes place, the immensity of God's love for us is encountered in the process. Fulton Sheen said, "There are two ways of knowing how *good* God is: one is never to lose Him through the preservation of innocence; the other is to find Him again after He has been lost."[2] We cannot but recognise Christ's mercy as a powerful expression of His love for us. This is why Jesus said, "The one to whom little is forgiven, loves little,"[3] because, in one sense, those who have experienced less of God's mercy have thereby experienced less of His love. Some of the great saints such as St Mary Magdalene, St Augustine, and

---

[1] cf. *CCC,* nos. 1855, 1856.

[2] *These are the Sacraments,* p. 78.

[3] Lk 7:47.

St Margaret of Cortona started off as great sinners. Much of their growth in sanctity can be attributed to the tremendous experience of His love that they encountered in His mercy.

Julian of Norwich, an English mystic of the Fourteenth Century, stated unashamedly that we need to realise that we need to sin. She was not encouraging sin, of course, but it was her way of saying that if we never fell, we would never know how weak we are, nor would we ever appreciate the astonishing love of God. She also said, "By the simple fact that we fall, we shall gain a deeper knowledge of what God's love means." Moreover, according to St Peter Chrysologus (406-450), when we give to God our sins which have injured and wounded His Son, we come to know God as our *Father*, for He gives us His goodness and a deeper love in return.[4] Even if we have no mortal sins to confess, going to Confession regularly with good dispositions can provide us with an increase of the virtue of charity. We can also see how our love for God grows through this sacrament on account of St James' words: "Draw near to God and he will draw near to you."[5]

Questions for Personal Reflection or Group Discussion

Alexander Pope said, "To err is human, to forgive divine." Does receiving divine mercy put you more in touch with the love of God?

What do you think of Julian of Norwich's statement: "We need to realise that we need to sin"?

[4] cf. Sermon 108.

[5] Jas 4:8.

Chapter Eighteen

It Fosters a Growth in Humility

There are no points for guessing how the frequent reception of the Sacrament of Reconciliation helps us to grow in humility. While confessing our sins can cause anxiety on one hand, it is encouraging to know that the humility it fosters provides five worthwhile benefits on the other. Firstly, without humility we could not acknowledge our own sinfulness, nor could we bring ourselves before God to plead for His aid.

Secondly, as St John Chrysostom said, humility "is the mother, the root, the nurse, and the fulcrum of every other virtue." St Teresa of Avila understood this well for she said, "While we are on this earth nothing is more important to us than humility."[1] She held the conviction that, together with love of neighbour and detachment from all created things, humility provided an important disposition necessary for prayer. She considered that these dispositions are so necessary that without them, being a good contemplative is impossible.[2] Although she spoke of humility last, she identified it as "the main practice" as it "embraces all others."[3]

Thirdly, humility can induce God to dwell within us and possess us more deeply. St Teresa explains this well:

> *There's no queen like humility for making the King to surrender. Humility drew the King from Heaven to the womb of the Virgin, and with it, by one hair we will draw Him to our souls. And realise that the one who has more humility will be the one who possesses Him more; and the one who has less will possess Him less. For I cannot understand how there could be humility without love or love without humility.*[4]

---

[1] *The Interior Castle* I, ch. 2, no. 9.

[2] *The Way of Perfection,* ch. 4, no. 3.

[3] *Ibid,* ch. 4, no. 4.

In saying that "there's no queen like humility," St Teresa had a chess board in mind. The queen is the most powerful figure and without it you will most likely lose the game! She also acknowledges that "the pain of genuine humility doesn't agitate or afflict the soul; rather, this humility expands it and enables it to serve God more."[5] She knew that without this virtue we would not be able to have knowledge of ourselves in the presence of God who loves us.[6] She not only saw that humility allows us to see ourselves as God see us, but that it even allows us to experience the delight that God experiences in us![7]

Fourthly, since pride is, as St Thomas Aquinas calls it, "the beginning of all sin"[8] and the "queen and mother of all the vices,"[9] confessing our sins gives us the opportunity to exercise the virtue that directly counteracts it. It thereby helps us to form good habits to overcome sin at its roots.

Fifthly, as St James tells us, "God opposes the proud, but gives grace to the humble."[10] In other words, the more humble we are, the more graces we receive from God. It follows that nothing facilitates a growth in grace as well as Confession, because in addition to dispensing God's grace, it fosters the humility we need to receive it. Knowing this can indeed make us less anxious about going to Confession. Jesus told St Faustina:

> *Tell souls that from this fount of mercy souls draw graces solely with the vessel of trust. If their trust is great, there is no limit to My generosity. The torrents of grace inundate humble souls. The proud remain always in poverty and misery, because My grace turns away from them to humble souls.*[11]

---

[4] *Ibid,* ch. 16, no. 2.
[5] *Ibid,* ch. 39, no. 2.
[6] cf. *The Interior Castle* I, ch. 3, nos. 8-9.
[7] cf. *Ibid,* I, ch. 1, no. 1.
[8] *Summa Theologica,* II-II, q. 162, art. 7; I-II, q. 84, art. 2.
[9] *Ibid* II-II, q. 162, art. 8.
[10] Prov 3:34; Jas 4:6; 1 Pet 5:5.
[11] *Divine Mercy in my Soul: Diary of Sister M. Faustina Kowalska*, no. 1602.

Since humility provides us with these, and so many other benefits revealed in the Scriptures,[12] we would do well to take the opportunity to exercise this virtue more often in Confession. Our muscles become stronger when we exercise them. Likewise, we grow in humility when we exercise this virtue in Confession. St Francis de Sales considered that this sacrament strengthens more than humility alone for he said, "In the single act of confession you will exercise more virtues than in any other act whatsoever."[13]

Questions for Personal Reflection or Group Discussion

Have you experienced the five benefits of humility outlined in this chapter?

Other than Confession, do you think there is any better way to grow in humility?

Do you agree with St Francis de Sales when he said, "In the single act of confession you will exercise more virtues than in any other act whatsoever"?

[12] The Scriptures tell us that humility induces God to: *listen* (cf. 2 Chr 7:14; Dan 10:12; Ps 138:6); *look at us* (cf. Isa 66:2; Sir 11:12) ; *forgive* (cf. 2 Chr 7:14); *deliver His people from evil* (cf. 2 Chr 36:12; Ps 18:27); *save us* (cf. Job 22:29); *make His people prosper* (cf. Sir 7:17; Prov 22:4); *lead us in what is right and teach us His way* (cf. Ps 25:9); *take pleasure in His people and adorn them with victory* (cf. Ps 149:4); *show His favour* (cf. Prov 3:34; Sir 3:18); *dwell within us* (cf. Isa 57:15); *come to us* (cf. Dan 10:12); *exalt us* (cf. Job 5:11; Esth 11:11; Sir 10:14; 11:1,12; Mt 23:12; Lk 1:52; 14:8 11; 18:14; Jas 4:10; 1 Pet 3:8; 5:6); *save us from punishment* (cf. Sir 7:17; Prov 22:4); and *make us the greatest in His kingdom* (cf. Mt 18:4). Furthermore, humility is said to be *God's delight* (cf. Sir 1:27). By humility *you will be loved by those whom God accepts.* (Sir 1:27). It enables us to *glorify God* (cf. Sir 3:20; Lk 1:46-48), *hear God and be glad* (cf. Ps 34:2), and *grow in wisdom* (cf. Prov 11:2). It brings us *honour* (cf. Prov 29:23); and the *prayer of the humble pierces the clouds, and it will not rest until it reaches its goal; it will not desist until the Most High responds* (Sir 35:21).

[13] St Francis de Sales, *Introduction to the Devout Life,* Part 2, ch. 19.

Chapter Nineteen

Growth in Self-knowledge

Why is self-knowledge so important? If you were not in the habit of checking your skin regularly and you developed a melanoma in an obscure place, you may not find it until it is too late. Self-knowledge is likewise important because although God's grace is able to help us, if we are ignorant of our own weaknesses, such blindness means that we simply do not go looking for God's help. In speaking of the importance of self-knowledge, St Teresa of Avila said:

> *Knowing ourselves is something so important that I wouldn't want any relaxation ever in this regard, however high you may have climbed into the Heavens.*[1] *I think one day of humble self-knowledge a greater favour from the Lord, even though the day may have cost us numerous afflictions and trials, than many days of prayer.*[2]

Here we can see that the Sacrament of Reconciliation affords us yet another benefit. Since we need to examine our conscience before we confess our sins, it conditions us to face ourselves, a habit which helps us grow in our self-knowledge. Examining our conscience has benefits of its own as we will see in the following chapter.

[1] *The Interior Castle,* I, ch. 2, no. 9.

[2] *The Foundations,* ch. 5, no. 16.

Questions for Personal Reflection or Group Discussion

Do you think the fast pace in which we live our lives today to a certain extent impedes our ability to grow in self-knowledge?

Do you think you would be aware of your strengths and weaknesses as much as you are if you were not in the habit of going to Confession?

Chapter Twenty

It Helps us to Form our Conscience

Our conscience is like a compass insofar as it helps us find our way to God. However, just as we will be mistaken about our route if we use a compass that is out of kilter, we are likely to make wrong decisions if our conscience is misguided. While we must not deliberately work against our conscience,[1] it nevertheless needs to be *informed.*[2] Without doing so it can misguide us due to ignorance and erroneous judgments. Therefore, we do well to be conscientious about informing our conscience. As we look at the potential pitfalls of a misguided conscience below, we will see that going to Confession not only purifies our conscience, it also informs it in the process.

Conscience and Guilt

It is not uncommon for guilt to be passed off as a negative thing today. Guilt is the objective fact that we have done something wrong and 'feeling guilty' is the subjective emotion associated with it. These are good if they move us to repentance and help prevent us from doing wrong in the future. As Fulton Sheen said:

> *If I am blind and deny there is any such thing as light, will I ever want to see? If I am deaf and deny there is any such thing as harmony, will I ever want to hear? If I am a sinner and deny there is any such thing as guilt, will I ever be forgiven?*[3]

Our sense of guilt and our guilty feelings are only negative when they are disproportionate to what we have actually done or do not move us to an appropriate response, as when people have 'morbid guilt' or 'scrupulosity.'

---

[1] St Paul knew the importance of obeying our conscience because if we reject it long enough we can lose all sense of sin: "By rejecting conscience, certain persons have made shipwreck of their faith" (1 Tim 1:19).
[2] cf. *CCC,* no. 1783.
[3] Talk given in a retreat to the priests of the diocese of Gary, Indiana, USA, 1973.

Guilt is often confused with shame. Shame is the objective fact of doing what is degrading or unworthy and 'feeling ashamed' is the subjective emotion associated with it. A person who 'has no shame' or is 'shameless' lacks a sense of their human dignity or does not feel the seriousness of what he has done, and may be a danger to others. Of any un-repented mortal sin we *should* feel appropriate shame. But shame can be a negative emotion if it is irrational, excessive or simply reflects wounded pride. If we feel ashamed because we thought, "How did I let *that* happen? I was so far *above* that to begin with!", then we do not truly know ourselves; if our shame is mere embarrassment that others know what wrong we have done, then it is for the wrong reasons; if our shame moves us to try to make excuses for ourselves, it is dishonest. A good confessor can help us keep our guilt and shame properly 'in synch' and appropriate to the facts of what we have done.

Ignorance and Responsibility

The Church teaches that if a person tries to rationalise his sins, making them out to be reasonable and right for himself – without trying to inform his conscience – he can actually be thereby adding to the seriousness of his sins: "Feigned ignorance and hardness of heart do not diminish, but rather increase the voluntary character of sin."[4] On this point George Cardinal Pell, the Archbishop of Sydney, said:

> *Ignorance of the law is no defense if we are prosecuted before a judge or magistrate. Is God like this or can we make an honest mistake? God judges what is in our hearts ... Nevertheless, moral blindness is possible. If we do not want to know the truth or refuse to make an effort to find out the facts, then God will hold us responsible for the consequent mistakes.*[5]

The only time a person is not culpable for following his erroneous conscience is when such error is due to "*invincible ignorance,*" that is, an ignorance that exists due to limited or no means to access the truth, or factors that impede the ability to perceive the truth, such as psychological, emotional and intellectual limitations or disabilities.

[4] *CCC,* no. 1859.

[5] *Issues of Faith and Morals* (San Francisco, 1999), p. 7.

Erroneous Conscience and Culpability

If our conscience misleads us we can still be culpable for the evil we commit, because, as the Church teaches:

> *This ignorance can often be imputed to personal responsibility. This is the case when a man takes little trouble to find out what is true and good, or when conscience is by degrees almost blinded through the habit of committing sin. In such cases, the person is culpable for the evil he commits. Ignorance of Christ and his Gospel, bad example given by others, enslavement to one's passions, assertions of a mistaken notion of autonomy of conscience, rejection of the Church's authority and her teaching, lack of conversion and of charity: these can be at the source of errors of judgment in moral conduct.*[6]

As educated Catholics we have little excuse for not being able to form our conscience. For if we read the quote above again we will be further convinced that the Sacrament of Reconciliation is a formidable means by which we can overcome many of the things which cause our judgment of moral conduct to become erroneous.

Blinded Conscience and Conversion

As we have seen, genuine guilt is the "friend" of conscience. If a person feels guilty it is usually a good sign. It means that he does not lack humility and that his conscience is healthy. When understood and used properly, it reminds us that our moral life is not in tune with objective moral truth. In turn, it enables us to seek reconciliation with God and our neighbours. Conversely, failing to make good use of the Sacrament of Reconciliation can result in a *blinded* conscience. This is found in those who – despite knowing what is morally wrong – consistently choose not to follow their conscience to such an extent that it loses its power to guide them. That is, their consistent dissent from their conscience desensitizes its ability to convict them of sin. On this point St Alphonsus said, "Bad actions naturally produce a certain shame; but this feeling is destroyed by the habit of sin."[7] Fulton Sheen also has a good way of explaining this:

---

[6] *CCC,* nos. 1791, 1792.

[7] Sermon 20.

> *It is a fact of human experience that the more experience we have of sin – our own sin – the less we are conscious of it. In all other things, we learn by experience; in sin, we unlearn by experience. Sin gets into the blood, the nerve cells, the brain, the habits, the mind; and the more it penetrates a person, the less he knows of its existence. The sinner becomes so accustomed to sin that he fails to recognise its gravity.*[8]

This is something we do well to be aware of today because many people are known to give greater priority to what they see to be pragmatic and expedient rather than to what their consciences dictate. This mind-set disposes many people to excuse themselves from their consciences when they have deliberately breached the Commandments. For example: "God will understand that I am living with my boyfriend because we love each other." Or, "It is just not practical to go to Mass *every* Sunday!" It follows that going to Confession often can prevent us from suffering from a blinded conscience because insofar as this sacrament facilitates and fosters repentance, our hearts are less likely to become hardened by an attachment to sin.

The Importance of a Truth-Informed Conscience

Of course the help we receive to inform our conscience will not do us much good if our understanding of the "primacy of conscience" is misguided. Some people mistakenly think that their conscience has primacy over everything else when they are faced with a moral dilemma. Others are a bit more careful and speak of the "primacy of an informed conscience." While we must always follow our conscience, if it permits things that are evil, we are still morally culpable because the sin lies at another stage in the process of moral discernment. The important point is that as Catholics we are not without the means to properly inform our conscience. The Church is no less equipped to guide us than Christ Himself because Jesus said to His apostles:

> *He who hears you hears me, and he who rejects you rejects me, and he who rejects me rejects him who sent me.*[9]

---

[8] *Peace of Soul,* p. 69.

[9] Lk 10:16.

This gives us further reason to be confident in the Church's teaching on faith and morals, especially when you consider that Jesus called the Holy Spirit who would teach us all things "the Spirit of Truth."[10] That is why St Paul was confident enough to even say that "we have the mind of Christ"[11] and that the Church is "the pillar and bulwark of the truth."[12] Thus, the Second Vatican Council taught that when we follow the teachings of the pope and bishops, we are following "not the mere word of men, but truly the word of God [1 Thes 2:13]."[13]

For those who love the Church, it is only natural then that they experience great assurance in seeking counsel from a priest whose words convey the mind and voice of Christ. Conversely, those who find themselves in real-life situations that require moral strength, honesty, and accuracy would be disappointed in receiving advice such as, "Just go with your conscience," or, "It is all up to you." Such a response would also leave them feeling isolated and deprived of guidance. Conversely, penitents are often grateful when they receive clear direction and guidance because it is often their desire to stay on the "straight and narrow" path which draws them to go to Confession.

Informing our Conscience

The Church teaches that, in order to form our conscience, we need to examine it, seek the guidance of the Church, the advice of competent people, the help of the Holy Spirit and His gifts, and employ the virtue of prudence.[14] Knowing this, why would we not want to receive the Sacrament of Reconciliation regularly given that all of these ways of forming our conscience converge in the process of making a good Confession? Especially when we consider that a well formed conscience "prevents or cures fear, selfishness and pride, resentment arising from guilt, and feelings of complacency, born of human weakness and faults." It "guarantees freedom and engenders peace of heart."[15]

---

[10] Jn 16:13.

[11] 1 Cor 2:16.

[12] 1 Tim 3:15.

[13] cf. *Lumen Gentium,* no. 12. See also *CCC,* nos. 888-892.

[14] *CCC,* nos. 1785, 1788.

[15] *CCC,* no. 1784.

Further help to form our conscience can be gained by asking the priest questions. If you ever find yourself in doubt regarding any concerns, relationships, moral issues, or to what degree a particular kind of desire, thought, action, or omission is sinful or not, he should be able to advise you, or refer you to someone who can. Sometimes we can think a particular action is not sinful, but in reality it is – or vice-a-versa. In all these things our confessor can help us to inform our conscience. This not only prevents confusion, but more importantly, it can help us to stay in the grace of God. St Paul knew that our conscience may not always be correct because he said:

> *I do not even judge myself. I am not aware of anything against myself, but I am not thereby acquitted. It is the Lord who judges me.* [16]

So asking our confessor anything we are unsure about helps us to "tune in" to what God is telling us, not just to avoid sin, but to be enthused about doing good! And since we are living in what Pope John Paul II has called the "era of new evangelization,"[17] regular Confession can help us to live our lives in ways which represent the Good News with greater integrity, appeal and attraction.

Conscience and Christ

Examining our conscience is not just a matter of introspection (that is, looking inwardly as we examine ourselves). That could easily lead to self-pity or scruples. Since we are examining ourselves in relation to God's love for us, such an examination best begins not with ourselves, but with Christ. There is no better way to know what sin truly is. For instance, how do we know what dirty water is? When we see and taste clean water. Or how do we know what a dissonant note in music is? When we know harmony. Likewise, if our focus is on Christ, we know, much

---

[16] 1 Cor 4:3-4.

[17] *On the Permanent Validity of the Church's Missionary Mandate (Redemptoris Missio)*, no. 3. All countries have been evangelised, but there is a need for *re-evangelisation* in countries where secularism, consumerism and atheism have brought about an indifference to God.

better than by any other means what sin is. St Teresa of Avila knew this well, for she said:

> *In my opinion we shall never completely know ourselves if we don't strive to know God. By gazing at His grandeur, we get in touch with our own lowliness; by looking at His purity, we shall see our own filth; by pondering His humility, we shall see how far we are from being humble … So I say, daughters, that we should set our eyes on Christ, our Good, and on His saints. There we shall learn true humility, the intellect will be enhanced, as I have said, and self-knowledge will not make one base and cowardly.*[18]

In short, the more we grow in our knowledge and love of Christ, the more we realise just how much we are not like Him. This is why those who go to Confession regularly are often able to recognise numerous areas in their lives for potential growth, whereas those who have infrequent recourse to this sacrament are often unable to identify any room for improvement. In fact, they can often say, "I have no sins to confess." So, since we need to examine our conscience before we go to Confession, one of the most positive benefits we receive from this practice is that it enables us to discover more opportunities to come closer to God. In view of all the benefits we have seen above, it stands to good reason that the Church recommends us to go to Confession regularly to help us form our conscience.[19]

---

[18] *The Interior Castle,* 1, ch. 2, nos. 9,11.

[19] cf. *CCC,* no. 1458.

Questions for Personal Reflection or Group Discussion

Does understanding how guilt is not to be confused with shame help you to see it as something positive?

Have you heard people refer to the primacy of conscience as if morality is relative, that is, that right and wrong behaviour are subjectively determined by each individual?

Do you use the Sacrament of Reconciliation as an opportunity to inform your conscience by asking your confessor questions and seeking his advice?

Chapter Twenty-One

Psychological Benefits

Peace of Soul

Peace of soul is a common psychological benefit of Confession because it brings serenity to our conscience. As Fulton Sheen said, all nature suggests an unburdening of oneself. Just as bodily ailments such as a boil, a bad tooth, or pus in a wound causes more pain if not removed, our sins can bring more pain to our conscience if they are not confessed. Just as our hand will go to our eye to provide relief from a speck, so the tongue will come to the aid of the heart to secure relief. As Shakespeare put it, "My tongue will tell the anger of mine heart, Or else my heart, concealing it, will break."[1] More importantly, sacramental confession is beneficial for our soul in the same way that our stomach vomits harmful substances from itself for the general good of our body.[2] Today, the irony is, as many Catholics have dropped going to Confession, the world has picked it up. Numerous television shows and talk-back radio stations now have "confess all" segments where people are asked to make public confessions! This demonstrates the deep underlying need we have to confess what would otherwise weigh heavy on our conscience.

Encouragement to Persevere

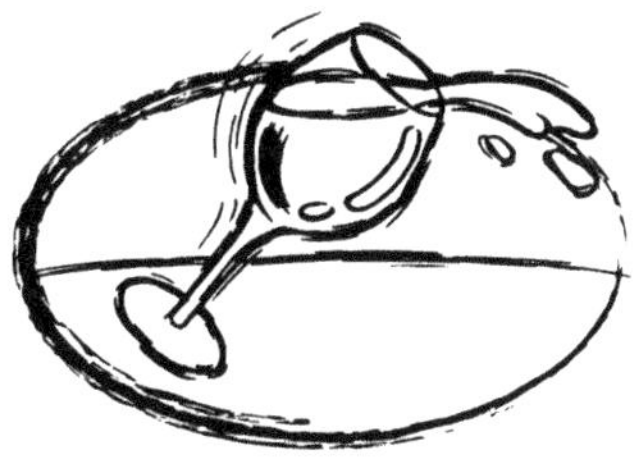

We can actually profit from the peace of soul that this sacrament affords. When a person soils a white shirt, his desire to preserve it from being further soiled can be diminished to such an extent that he could not care less about soiling it again. Likewise, when we sin, we can often think, "I've done it now. I might as well keep sinning." The

[1] *The Taming of the Shrew,* Act 4, Scene 3.

[2] cf. *These are the Sacraments,* pp. 67, 74.

consequence of this attitude is unfortunate because temporal punishment accumulates with every individual sin, including a venial sin.[3] However, when he washes the cloth, the joy of knowing that it is clean increases his desire to keep it clean. Likewise, the more often we go to Confession, the more often we renew our desire to grow closer to God. In short, it exercises our desire to improve our spiritual life.

If this is unapparent to them, this is true for those who keep confessing the same sins. Sometimes people express that they feel like a hypocrite for confessing the same sins time and time again, not through any lack of contrition or desire for amendment on their part, but through human weakness. What I would tell them is this: "Do you know what the basic definition of a hypocrite is? A hypocrite is someone who knows what is morally good but does not try to live up to it. The mere fact that you want to be reconciled with God means that you are most likely *not* a hypocrite because by confessing your sins you are distancing yourself from what is wrong and aspiring to what you know to be good."

It Can Prevent Psychological Disturbances

Perhaps our appreciation of the Sacrament of Reconciliation would be greater if it was more widely known that it can prevent the onset of psychological disturbances. How? Why? When a person rationalises away his sins, they are thrust down into his unconsciousness, but somehow they re-emerge and make themselves felt in his mental attitudes (such as low self-esteem or even self-hatred), and his general outlook on life. Subsequently they can bring about ill health. Fulton Sheen explains:

> *Suppress a sin, and it becomes buried, and later on will come out in complexes. It is very much like keeping the cap on a tube of toothpaste. If one submits it to great pressure, the toothpaste will come out somewhere; one does not know where. The normal place for it to come out is through the top. So too, if we suppress our guilt or deny it, we put our mind under pressure and it creates abnormalities. The guilt does not come out where it ought to be, namely, in the sacrament.*[4]

[3] cf. *CCC,* no. 1863.

[4] *These are the Sacraments,* p. 74.

According to this understanding, Sheen said that fear, when it is born of guilt, can sometimes bring about a mental disturbance. That is, a fear of guilt, and the guilt that is engendered by fear is known to beget neurosis and psychosis. He does not give any detailed explanation of the difference between neurosis and psychosis, but in his own humorous way he explains it this way: "The difference is partly this. Every neurotic person *dreams* about living in castles in Spain; every psychotic person *lives* in castles in Spain, and the psychiatrist often collects rent from both!"[5] Although all mental disturbances do not come from guilt he said that there are more that come from guilt than is generally suspected because there never is *repression* without an *expression*. He gives an example of this by telling the following true story:

> *There was an authentic case that was revealed and told to an English psychiatrist: During the war a British soldier one night jumped over his trench. He went into a trench of three German soldiers, and bayoneted them. He was seen by his commanding officer who raised him in rank immediately. He ordered a medal to be given to him. When he returned to London he was praised and feted. But, there was something that happened that no one knew about: the three German soldiers were already so badly wounded they could not fight back. So this English soldier repressed the guilt more and more. And he was torn between the love of praise and the affirmation of his ego, and the dread of being discovered. And so he said to himself, "Well, if I never told anyone about it, and if I never talked in my sleep, who would know?" So he told no one about it and he never talked in his sleep.* **And became dumb!** *He could not speak. A psychiatrist, however, plunged, and found out the reason for it. But this submerging of guilt had produced this particular neurosis. And so it is, with many today who are suffering from mental disturbances – not all, because there are a hundred other causes – but guilt is one of the principal reasons for these mental errancies.*[6]

With this understanding it is not hard to see why Sheen came to the conclusion that: "Regular Confession prevents our sins, our worries, our fears, our anxieties from seeping into the unconscious and denigrating

---

[5] Fulton J Sheen, *Life is Worth Living*, "Psychology of Fear" (Soundtrack of TV Broadcast).
[6] *Ibid.*

into melancholy, psychosis, and neurosis."[7] This view is also held by psychologists.[8] This is no recent discovery. For example, in 1960 Albert Ellis wrote in one leading psychology journal that sin can cause people to become psychologically disturbed[9], while in the same year O Hobart Mowrer wrote in another leading journal that psychologists have "cut the very roots of [their] being" by disregarding sin.[10]

It can Prevent Depression

Dr John Poon, a psychologist of Sydney, said that if more Catholics had recourse to the Sacrament of Reconciliation, fewer Catholics would suffer from depression. This is a remarkable statement, especially since he said, "Depression is the number one top public health problem and its increase is shocking."[11] It is interesting to hear a psychologist say that "there is an antidote to depression in the sacraments, especially the Eucharist and Reconciliation, and in Scripture, especially the Ten Commandments and the Beatitudes."[12] In saying this, he did not say that Confession should be seen as a substitute for medical attention and cognitive therapy for those who are suffering from depression.

We can understand why psychologists, such as Dr Poon, are saying that this sacrament is a formidable antidote to depression because sin can make us discouraged and depressed! This is especially true if guilt is not confessed but repressed. Much of modern culture is directed to the suppression of our discontent. This suppression manifests itself in the widespread use of sleeping tablets, drugs, alcohol, and the constant search for pleasures. As the loss of the sense of sin has become so widespread in our society, it could be readily assumed that many people are suffering inner turmoil and discontent, "burning their fingers" as it were through sin. This could be one of the causes of the increasing suicide rates because

---

[7] *Peace of Soul,* p. 140.

[8] cf. *Professional Psychology: Research and Practice (American Psychological Association)*, 37(3), June 2006, pp. 295–302.

[9] cf. A Ellis (1960), *There is no place for the concept of sin in psychotherapy (Journal of Counseling Psychology)*, 7, p. 192.

[10] O H Mowrer, (1960), *"Sin," the lesser of two evils. (American Psychologist)*, 15, p. 303.

[11] *Catholic Weekly,* Sydney, 10 July 2005, p. 5.

[12] *Ibid.*

they are increasing in the same regions where there is a growing loss of the sense of sin.

Since there are so many benefits that can be received from going to Confession, it is not difficult to understand why this sacrament has received a growing empirical support among psychologists.[13] Many also deem spiritual resources for healing as important.[14]

Questions for Personal Reflection or Group Discussion

Do you think you could attain the same extent of peace of soul without the Sacrament of Reconciliation?

Is the analogy of the white table cloth something you can relate to?

Does it surprise you to hear what psychologists are saying about Confession?

[13] cf. J W Pennebaker, C F Hughes, & R C O'Heeron (1987), *The psychophysiology of confession: Linking inhibitory and psychosomatic processes (Journal of Personality and Social Psychology)*, 52, pp. 781-793.

[14] cf. S Y Tan, *Religion in clinical practice: Implicit and explicit integration,* In E P Shafranske (Ed.), *Religion and the clinical practice of psychology* (Washington, DC: American Psychological Association., 1996), pp. 365-387.

Chapter Twenty-Two

It Prevents us From Falling into More Serious Sins

Our own experience tells us that one sin can often lead to another. For example, pride can lead to jealousy, jealousy to envy, envy to anger, and so on. Sins that are committed in our mind can lead us to commit sins in word and action. Sins committed out of weakness can lead to sins of malice. Little by little, venial sins can lead to mortal sins.[1] What is more, sin tends to reproduce itself and reinforce itself. St Thomas Aquinas explains one of the reasons for this. So long as a person remains unreconciled to God, he cannot long abstain from committing some new sin because he is deprived of sanctifying grace.[2] Furthermore, if sins are not confessed but repressed; if they are concealed rather than revealed, they can begin to take more of a hold on us because problems grow and become more established in the dark. For this reason, if a person cannot talk about something then it is likely that it is already out of control in his life. However, when he exposes his struggles to the light of truth, they can often shrink and lose their tenacity.

It follows, therefore, that a timely Confession can prevent us from falling into more serious sins. It can also help us to enjoy a greater freedom to grow in virtue. Here the saying which refers to repairing torn fabric, "A stitch in time saves nine" is understood at its best. On this note St Alphonsus asks a poignant question:

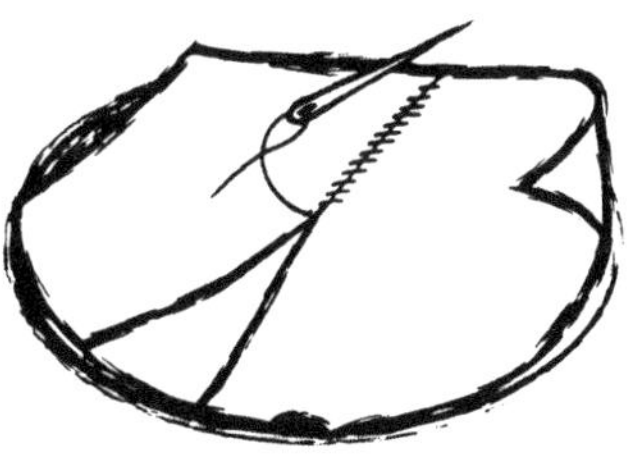

[1] cf. *CCC,* no. 1863.

[2] cf. *Summa Theologica,* II-II, q. 109, art. 8.

> *My brother, if you cannot now break the cords by which you are at present bound, will you be able to break them hereafter, when they shall be doubled by the commission of new sins?*[3]

If we wait until we have major sins to confess before we go to Confession we would not be benefiting from this sacrament as best we could. St Teresa of Avila said that a good Confession will not only save us from further harm, but that it could even transform what the devil intends for our downfall into our greater good:

> *But if one proceeds with humility, strives to know the truth, is subject to a confessor, and communicates with him openly and truthfully, it will come about, as has been said,*[4] *that the things by which the devil intends to cause death will cause life, however many the haunting illusions he wants to scare you with.*[5]

Questions for Personal Reflection or Group Discussion

Have you noticed how one sin can lead to another in your life?

Can you relate to what St Teresa of Avila said about making a good Confession and how it can transform what the devil intends for our downfall into our greater good?

[3] Sermon 52.
[4] cf. *The Way of Perfection,* ch. 38, nos. 3-4.
[5] *Ibid,* ch. 40, no. 4.

Chapter Twenty-Three

It Improves our Prayer Life

Human nature has it that whenever we are attached to sin, or at least *finite* things, we naturally derive less satisfaction from companionship from the One alone who is *Infinite*. Furthermore, it is a fundamental psychological law that we enjoy the presence of that which we love. If we love Christ, we will enjoy His presence, but if our life is not fully oriented to Christ, we can find it difficult to pray to Him. Our Lord Himself commented on this basic rule of human nature when He said, "Where your treasure is, there will your heart be also."[1] If our treasure is Christ, we will find it easier to centre our thoughts and affections on Him precisely because our heart is *in* Him, but if our treasure is in things other than Him, so too will our hearts be in those things, taking our focus away from Christ. If Christ is thereby no longer central to our desires, then why should we be surprised if we experience distractions, inner emptiness and dissatisfaction in prayer? The "pure of heart" do indeed "see God,"[2] and "the upright shall behold his face."[3]

Accordingly, if we are still involved in sin, or tepidity, or mediocrity, we are likely to encounter difficulties in overcoming distractions or some degree of aridity in prayer. This is especially true of contemplative prayer because it is a gift God gives only to the extent that we are conformed to His Son. Unlike meditation, contemplation involves not only our own mental efforts, but the activity of the Holy Spirit, such

[1] Mt 6:21.

[2] cf. Mt 5:8.

[3] Ps 11:7.

that it is called *infused* prayer (that is, produced in the soul by God). St Teresa understood this correlation between prayer and the wider fabric of life through her own experience:

> *Since His Majesty was not waiting for anything other than some preparedness in me, the spiritual graces went on increasing in the manner I shall tell. It is not a customary thing for the Lord to give them except to those with greater purity of conscience.*[4]

St Teresa knew this to be so true, that if humility, detachment from all created things, patience, temperance, chastity, love for neighbour, etc, are not growing, neither will the quality of our prayer life grow. She knew that contemplation is not simply a pious occupation that takes place in a chapel or in some other quiet place. Rather it is something which both *influences* and is *influenced by* the degrees to which we are taking discipleship seriously. Although our efforts to pray are primarily important, our love for God cannot be seen as something separate from love of neighbour, for as Christ told us:

> *So if you are offering your gift at the altar, and there remember that your brother has something against you, leave your gift there before the altar and go; first be reconciled to your brother, and then come and offer your gift.*[5]

In other words, if peace is lacking in the relationships we have with those who Christ calls us to see as our brothers and sisters, then it is only natural that we will not find peace in prayer.

Aridity in prayer does not always have its origins in our failure to centre our lives on Christ. It can also be caused by two other things: (i) involuntary circumstances such as tragic events, sickness, difficulty finding a good place to pray, noises, and other interruptions; and (ii) the purifying action of God. However, for the times our difficulties in prayer are attributed to our own personal sins and imperfections, the Sacrament of Reconciliation can be of great benefit to our prayer life. By purifying ourselves from these obstacles that we place between ourselves and God, it can often enable us to be more conscious of His presence and to enter more deeply into contemplation.

---

[4] *The Book of Her Life*, ch. 9, no. 9.

[5] Mt 5:23.

Questions for Personal Reflection or Group Discussion

Have you noticed that you usually pray better after going to Confession?

Does it help to understand that the quality of your prayer correlates with the degree to which you are taking discipleship seriously in the wider fabric of life?

Aridity in prayer does not always have its origins in failing to centre your life on Christ. When you think your time in prayer was not well spent, do you still persevere, trusting that God is nevertheless pleased with your desire to respond to His love?

Chapter Twenty-Four

Spiritual Direction

Encouragement and Advice

The Sacrament of Reconciliation provides us with the opportunity to receive words of advice and encouragement from the priest. Even if such spiritual guidance is brief, it can be very helpful in the spiritual life because it helps us to attain greater discretion, especially when we consider that it is hard to be objective when our own interests are involved. Our need for individual spiritual guidance is comparable to a person who has been in a closed room for a long time – he does not notice that the air has become stale, whereas one who comes in from the outside notices it immediately. This happens on account of how we often do not understand what is happening in our soul, for as the Prophet Jeremiah said, "The heart is deceitful above all things, and desperately corrupt; who can understand it?"[1] In light of this, spiritual direction can greatly assist us because it helps us to grow in our self-knowledge in the light of the Holy Spirit and to become more sensitive to God's presence and activity in our lives.

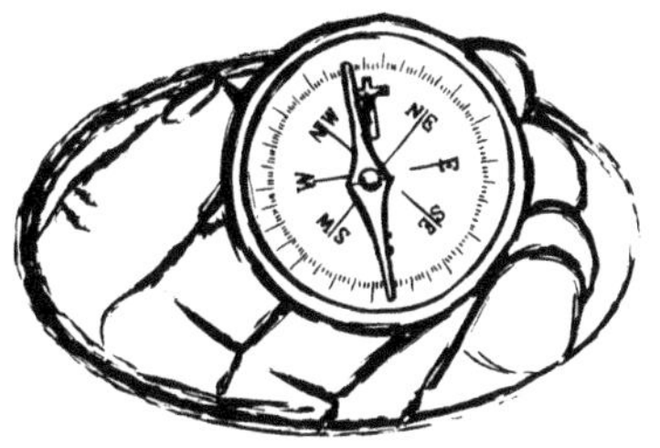

In addition to this, the priest's awareness of the many hidden obstacles in life that hinder union with God – his prayer life, his study of philosophy and theology, his knowledge of the Church's teachings and spiritual tradition, the lives of the saints and the wisdom of their words, and his own practice of the Christian virtues – can provide us with numerous insights. These can greatly assist our own efforts to pray and grow in our own knowledge and love of God.

[1] Jer 17:9.

It Fosters Objectivity in Discernment

Going to Confession frequently can also help us to discern our vocation because this practice predisposes us to view our life more in relation to God's will than our own immediate desires. Furthermore, the advice we receive can encourage us to take decisive steps. Such encouragement is often needed because the difficulties we face in discernment are not so much attributed to a *lack of clarity* in our calling but to a *weakness of will* in responding. Many of the great people we meet in the Bible had this difficulty. Their growth in sanctity was greatly assisted by the direction they received from others. For example, when God called Moses to lead his people out of their slavery in Egypt to the Promised Land, he was afraid, weak, and doubtful about his mission. He did not possess the courage to give strong credence to what God was calling him to do. However, this all changed when he was heartened by God through his brother, Aaron. God said to Moses:

> *Is there not Aaron, your brother, the Levite? I know that he can speak well; and behold, he is coming out to meet you, and when he sees you he will be glad in his heart. And you shall speak to him and put the words in his mouth; and I will be with your mouth and with his mouth, and will teach you what you shall do.*[2]

This is just one example from the Scriptures. There are many others, such as:

- the advice Moses received from his father-in-law, Jethro;[3]
- the encouragement Gideon received about the seemingly impossible mission God entrusted to him when he heard about a Midianite's dream;[4]
- the numerous times King David received encouragement and advice from the Prophet Nathan; and
- the confirmation Ananias gave to St Paul about his vision which enabled him to be "increased all the more in strength"[5] to become an Apostle of Christ.

---

2 Ex 4:14-15.
3 cf. Ex 18:1-27.
4 cf. Judg 7:13-15.
5 Acts 9:22.

As you can see, the inspirations and promptings of the Holy Spirit that enlighten, convict, and encourage us from *within* are more likely to achieve their desired effect if they are confirmed from *without*. This confirmation we receive from our confessor can provide great help, for as St John of the Cross said, "Until consulting another, one will usually experience only tepidity and weakness in the truth, no matter how much may have been heard from God."[6]

Questions for Personal Reflection or Group Discussion

Has the spiritual direction you have received in Confession helped you?

Do you ask your confessor for guidance in matters of uncertainty?

[6] *The Ascent of Mt Carmel,* Bk II, ch. 22, no. 12.

Chapter Twenty-Five

It Helps us to Become Saints

We are all called to be saints, but it is only possible by the grace of God. Since this sacrament restores so much grace within us – the very assistance we need to grow in holiness – it is a pity that it has suffered so much neglect in recent years. Given our understanding of the many benefits we receive in this sacrament, those who have distanced themselves from Confession should not be surprised, despite many of their own human efforts, if they have been failing to overcome vice and grow in virtue. Conversely, the following words Our Lord said to St Veronica Juliani confirm what we have learned in the previous chapters:

> *You shall make progress in perfection in proportion to the fruits which you shall draw from this sacrament.*[1]

Pope John Paul II made similar statements:

> *I do not hesitate to say that even the great canonized saints are generally the fruit of those confessionals.*[2]
>
> *It would be an illusion to seek after holiness, according to the vocation one has received from God, without partaking frequently of this sacrament of conversion and reconciliation. Those who go to Confession frequently, and do so with the desire to make progress, will notice the strides that they make in their spiritual lives.*[3]

The benefits articulated above are available to all Catholics without exception, for Jesus said to St Faustina, "The greatest sinners would achieve great sanctity, if only they would trust in My mercy."[4]

---

[1] Cited in Fr Reginald Garrigou Lagrange, OP, *The Three Ages of the Interior Life*, p. 404.

[2] *Reconciliatio et Paenitentia*, no. 29.

[3] Address to participants in a Conference of the Apostolic Penitentiary, Rome, 27 March 2004.

[4] *Divine Mercy in my Soul: Diary of Sister M. Faustina Kowalska*, no. 1784.

Questions for Personal Reflection or Group Discussion

Can you relate to what Our Lord said to St Veronica Juliani?

Is it encouraging to learn, as Pope John Paul II said, "that even the great canonized saints are generally the fruit of those confessionals"?

Conclusion

By studying the numerous benefits that the Sacrament of Reconciliation provides us, we have more than enough reason to see how privileged we are as Catholics. This sacrament is indeed a great gift. If there is one thing that these twenty-five benefits have in common, it is this: This sacrament does not just free us from sin. Salvation is more than that. It also restores and increases our opportunities to share in God's divine life. Even while we are on earth, this sacrament enables us to anticipate the joy of being united with God in Heaven, because here and now, it makes our participation in His divine life possible. In turn, this enables us to enjoy "the glorious liberty of the children of God."[1] In other words, the Sacrament of Reconciliation does not just free us *from* vice; it also gives us freedom *for* virtue. Likewise, it does not just liberate us *from* sin; it also provides freedom *for* holiness.

This approach to the Sacrament of Reconciliation helps us to see that it is a gift, not a burden. Emphasizing the benefits and blessings of Confession is a welcome alternative to presenting this sacrament as the spiritual equivalent of a trip to the dentist. If it has been some time since you have been to the Sacrament of Reconciliation I hope you now have more reasons to look forward to receive God's pardon and peace. If you prefer to remain anonymous, many parishes still have the screen within the confessional box which prevents you from being seen. Furthermore, if the times for Confession in your local parish are not convenient, you can ask to receive this sacrament at any other time. Priests are often requested to make themselves available outside scheduled times, so you have no reason to think you are any cause of inconvenience.

The following words Jesus said to St Faustina provide further inspiration to those who may be hesitating in their response to His invitation: "Sooner would heaven and earth turn into nothingness than would My mercy not embrace a trusting soul."[2]

---

[1] cf. Rom 8:21.

[2] *Divine Mercy in my Soul: Diary of Sister M. Faustina Kowalska*, no. 1777.

Appendix A: What is Sin?

In chapter one, the forgiveness of sin was introduced without defining what sin is. Hence the following definition may be helpful to those who wish to understand what it essentially is.

Most people understand that a sin is something immoral. While this is true – sin is not simply about breaking a law, or harming ourselves or someone else – it is primarily about *offending God.* (God is offended by our sins because through them we choose ourselves, others, or things before or above Him who is deserving of all our love.) Nor are certain kinds of behaviour morally wrong because God forbids them. Rather, God forbids them because they are immoral.

By raising our awareness of sin, God also has our own good in mind. Properly understood, His Commandments do not place restrictions on us. Rather, they increase our freedom. When we are inconvenienced by traffic lights when driving we may at times think that they are restricting our freedom. We nevertheless consider the freedom they provide to travel safely as more precious. Likewise, by trying to follow God's Commandments we gain the precious freedom to choose Him, to love Him, and to participate in the eternal ecstasy of His divine life.

Since sin is a deliberate choice not to walk in God's ways it sounds reasonable to ask, "What makes God's ways better than my own?" To this we do well to see that God's ways are always ways of right relationship not only because "God is love"[1] but because God *is* relationship: He is a communion of Persons (Father, Son, and Holy Spirit). God has made us in His image and likeness (that is, to love one another according to the love found in the Holy Trinity.) So when we sin, we distort and misrepresent the image of God in which we are made as it filters out His love. This is at the heart of what sin is. It is an injustice to God not only because it involves a rejection but also a misrepresentation of His

[1] 1 Jn 4:16.

love. Jesus said to St Teresa of Avila, "everything that is displeasing to me is a lie."[2] When we sin, we violate the truth of who God made us to be: people made in His image and likeness. So when we go to Confession, in effect, we strip off our old self, and clothe ourselves anew in the image of God who created us.[3]

---

[2] *The Book of her Life,* ch. 40, no. 1.

[3] cf. Col 3:9-10.

Appendix B: Frequently Asked Questions about Confession

In chapter three we noted that people often ask, "Why do I need to confess my sins to a priest?" Here we will provide some assuring answers to this and other frequently asked questions which arise from the difficulties involved in going to Confession.

Why do I need to confess my sins to a priest?

The confession of sins is integral to the Sacrament of Reconciliation because when Christ entrusted this sacrament to His apostles He said:

> *"As the Father has sent me, even so I send you." And when he had said this, he breathed on them, and said to them, "Receive the Holy Spirit. If you forgive the sins of any, they are forgiven; if you retain the sins of any, they are retained."*[1]

These words imply that Christ expects sins to be confessed. How would the priests of the Church know which sins to forgive (by giving absolution) and which sins to retain (by not giving absolution) if they did not hear them? Since it is Christ who is forgiving sins through the ministry of the priest, the priest cannot do anything that Christ Himself cannot do, namely, absolve our sins if we are not sorry. Not being sorry means not believing what we did was wrong, or not having a firm purpose to avoid sin or the *occasions of sin* (persons, places, things, or any act that previously led us into sin or made us susceptible to sin). It is for this reason that the Church teaches that in order to receive absolution we must first confess all of our serious sins and the number of times we committed them (as far as we can remember) and allow the dispositions which make forgiveness possible to be examined, namely, our sorrow and firm purpose of amendment.[2]

---

[1] Jn 20:21-23. See also Mt 16:19.

[2] cf. *Council of Trent,* Session XIV, ch. 5; *Rite of Penance,* 6 b, 7 a; *Code of Canon Law,* 1983 *(CIC),* can. 988, §1; John Paul II, *On Certain Aspects of the Celebration of the Sacrament of Penance (Misericordia Dei),* nos. 1, 3; *DS* 1707.

During the lifetime of the Apostles we can see that Jesus' instructions about confessing sins were put into practice because both St John and St James tell us that those who confess their sins will receive God's forgiveness.[3] St James' words provide particular clarity because he prescribes "self-help" for everything other than sin. For example, he says, "Is anyone among you suffering? Let him pray."[4] But for the forgiveness of sins he said "presbyters" (priests) should be called upon.[5] This is consistent with what happened in the Old Testament:

> *...to the early Jewish converts to Christianity, the Sacrament of Penance did not appear as a startling innovation. A rite accompanied by confession of sin was one of the many Jewish practices which by divine ordinance passed quite naturally into the religious life of the New Israel, the Church. Under the Old Law, a sinner offered sacrifice for sin (Num 5:6-8), the priest decided according to the gravity of the sin – therefore after an avowal on the part of the repentant sinner – whether the victim presented was of sufficient value or not (Lev 5:10-11, 18; 6:2 7). When Jews confessed their sins before John the Baptist and were symbolically washed clean by him, there was no shock at the ritual; something like it was already a part of Jewish life, and was carried over into the new dispensation. A Jewish convert could see at once how the New Law fulfilled the Old: he still had to go to the priest and admit his guilt, and still had to hope for pardon in the blood of a Victim – no longer a beast of the herd, but the Lamb of God, offered once for all, possessing a power of propitiation available at every moment.*[6]

Another reason why we confess our sins to a priest can be found in chapter seven, under the subheading, *Sharing in Christ's Redemptive Work*.

But can't God forgive me *without* this sacrament?

God is not restricted to the sacraments in forgiving sins. We can receive God's forgiveness through a perfect act of contrition, especially at the point of death. However, we receive far more abundant graces from the sacraments than we would obtain by making the same acts without

[3] cf. Jas 5:16; 1 Jn 1:9.
[4] Jas 5:15.
[5] cf. Jas 5:14-15.
[6] Archbishop Michael Sheehan, *Apologetics and Catholic Doctrine*, revised & ed. by Fr P M Joseph (London, 2001), p. 552.

the sacraments because Christ Himself is at work in them. This is especially true of the Sacrament of Reconciliation because the Church teaches that *attrition* (imperfect contrition[7]) *outside* the Sacrament of Reconciliation – cannot obtain the forgiveness of mortal sins, whereas attrition is enough to dispose us to obtain God's forgiveness *in* Confession.[8] Knowing this can be very reassuring.

There is reason to believe that many are not aware of this because it is not uncommon for Catholics to say, "I don't need to go to Confession. I have told God in prayer that I am sorry. He has forgiven me already." While it is true that our venial sins can be forgiven by such means, it is complacent to think that our serious sins are forgiven through prayer alone because we can never be sure if we have perfect contrition for our sins. This does not mean we should not strive to have perfect contrition when we go to Confession because in chapter five we noted that the more perfectly disposed we are to this sacrament the more graces we receive.

What will the priest think of me if I confess this or that sin?

Since the priest is deeply humbled by his role of representing Christ sacramentally, he would be very insensitive if he had no desire to exemplify Christ's kindness and merciful compassion to his penitents. You may think, "Yes, I believe that I am confessing my sins to Christ, and I believe that it is Christ who is speaking to me when the priest says, "I absolve you from your sins," but what does the priest himself think of me? What will he think of me if I confess this or that sin?" Here you do well to remember that priests are not 'immune' to temptation and sin, for as St Paul said, a priest "can sympathise with those who are ignorant or uncertain because he too lives in the limitation of weakness."[9] Their

[7] Although *attrition* is a sorrow for sin prompted by the Holy Spirit and born of the consideration of sin's ugliness or the fear of eternal damnation, this degree of sorrow is inferior to perfect contrition. Sorrow is perfect when it is born of the consideration of God's love for us. Fear is associated with perfect contrition but unlike imperfect contrition it is not a servile fear but a filial one, that is, it is a fear that comes from not wanting to offend the one that we love rather than a fear of being punished.

[8] cf. *CCC,* no. 1453.

[9] Heb 5:2. (*JB*)

awareness of how humbling it is to confess their own sins enables them to identify with your need for an understanding and empathetic ear. St John Chrysostom suggested that this is why the Priesthood was not entrusted to the angels: for inasmuch as it is impossible for them to sin, they could be very severe and call down thunder and lightning on sinners! On the other hand, as fellow human beings, priests are more naturally inclined to be understanding due to the frailty we all experience, for as St Paul said, "No temptation has overtaken you that is not common to man."[10]

On this note, the "saint of Confession," St Leopold Mandic, OFM Cap (1866-1942), once asked, "Why should we humiliate any more souls which have come to prostrate themselves at our feet? Are they not humbled enough? Did Jesus humiliate the publican, the woman taken in adultery, the Magdalener?"[11] As a priest, he knew that the very fact penitents come to confess their sins means it can be assumed that they are in the right frame of mind.

We know from our own experience that it is not easy to acknowledge our faults. Consider some of the following reasons why being open can be difficult:

- *Mistaken beliefs:* Sometimes we can think that we are the only one in the world who sins, or at least that we are the only one who has the weaknesses that we have.
- *Embarrassment:* Sometimes we feel embarrassed and even full of shame about our weaknesses and sins.
- *Attachments:* Other times we are too attached to certain things or patterns of behaviour. Even though we want to be liberated from these bad habits, we lack the humility to ask for help.

---

[10] 1 Cor 10:13.

[11] P E Bernardi, *Leopoldo Mandic Saint of Reconciliation* (Padua, 1989), p. 235.

- *Fear:* We can be afraid that we will be misunderstood, that is, that we will misrepresent the good in us if we talk about our weaknesses, that we will thereby be judged unfairly, and that the priest will look down on us.

You would not be troubled so much by these thoughts and feelings if you knew that priests will *not* look down on you or think of you poorly. In fact, opening your soul to a priest only serves to deeply humble *him*! Speaking from my own experience, if you only knew just how much the priest is humbled by the amount of trust and confidence invested in him as a spiritual father, you would not be so anxious. Having stated this, however, the brutal truth is that not all priests are good confessors. If a priest has given you a negative experience of Confession, do not let it discourage you, and if necessary, find another confessor. Priests are only human and need our prayers.

In chapter three we considered how penitents are able to encounter Christ in the ministry of the priest. Have you ever considered that the priest encounters Christ too? You might think, "But the priest is the one who is called to represent Him, so what are you talking about?" It is precisely because the priest *is* called to represent Christ sacramentally that he encounters Him quite profoundly. While penitents may be inclined to be self-conscious, the priest is far more conscious of Christ's presence because he is deeply aware of his own unworthiness to represent Him through the Sacrament of the Priesthood. He is moved in awe and reverence because the confidence invested in him immediately puts him in touch with Christ; he is aware that Jesus is present in his poor humanity in that graced moment like a treasure in an earthenware vessel.[12]

The greater the trust and confidence invested, the more he is profoundly aware that Christ is 'filling his shoes.' This affiliation with the person and mission of Christ conforms him more closely to Jesus, even to the point whereby his love and care for those in need of mercy increases his desires to lay down his life in sacrifice for them. As we saw in chapter twelve, these desires have been known to burn so greatly in so many saintly priests such as St John Vianney, that for them no voluntary sacrifice seemed too big to offer to God to further assist the penitent's desire for

[12] cf. 2 Cor 4:7.

salvation. So confiding in a priest does not make him look down on anyone, it only makes him look *up* – up to Christ – and might I add, up to the penitents themselves, for their humble sincerity is a powerful manifestation of their own love for Christ and His mercy. This is clearly evident because the measure of our love for anything is the amount of pain we are willing to suffer to gain that which we love. Therefore, the greater shame or embarrassment we have in confessing our desire to be more united to God, the greater testimony we are giving to our love for Christ.

To sum up, in hearing your confession, priests take delight in the "new you", not the "old you." Since there is awe in seeing God's grace at work in such a tangible way, the confession of penitents readily boosts the morale of priests.

What if the priest knows me?

Most confessionals provide you with the option of kneeling before a screen which prevents you from being seen by the priest. You might consider, however, that being known by the priest is not altogether something to be afraid of for the following reasons: People sin against God and not the priest. Furthermore, since your parish priest hears so many confessions he will most likely forget what you confessed.

This may not be the case were you to go to Confession to the same priest frequently. However, this is actually something we do well to desire. You probably have a General Practitioner that you go to regularly – a doctor who knows you well – because in knowing you and your medical history and how various complaints can be related, he is able to provide a better diagnosis of your body's health. If we are open enough to see it, we would not want to act any differently with our spiritual health, especially when you consider that this is far more important than bodily health. Having considered that we should not be afraid to have a confessor who knows us, I am not referring to priests to whom you are related, or to those with whom you directly work. However, in general, having a regular confessor will mean that we will receive more helpful spiritual guidance in the long term.

Appendix C: Common Misunderstandings of Sin

In chapter four we looked at the misguided assertion: "There is no such thing as mortal sin." It may be helpful to know that the Church has corrected three other common misunderstandings:

Is a mortal sin only committed when one has a direct contempt for the love of God?

Some suppose that a mortal sin must involve a direct contempt for God (that is, a conscious hatred of Him). Since this seldom happens, those who think this do not think they have offended God when they have knowingly and willingly breached the Commandments in a major way. However, even those who are trying to love God can offend Him because sin takes place through an illusion, rationalisation, and self-deception.

For this reason the Congregation for the Doctrine of the Faith explained that a mortal sin can be committed by a seriously disordered action even when it does not come from a direct contempt for the love of God and neighbour. For by freely, consciously and deliberately choosing something seriously disordered, for whatever reason, one not only turns away from the Commandments but from God Himself and loses charity.[1]

Is there more than a twofold distinction of sins?

The Church has not always used the same words to describe mortal sin. Throughout history words such a *serious*, *grave*, and *mortal* have been used; but in using these words the Church has always referred to sin which is objectively mortal. Despite this, a common misunderstanding has evolved from those who have proposed that there is a "threefold distinction of sins, classifying them as venial, serious and mortal." Pope John Paul II

[1] cf. *Persona humana,* (1975), no. 10.

dismissed this proposal on the grounds that it attempts to make out that some sins which involve serious matter are mortal whereas others are not. Knowing that such a "scale" does not exist and that sin is either venial or mortal, he says:

> *But it still remains true that the essential and decisive distinction is between sin which destroys charity and sin which does not kill the supernatural life: There is no middle way between life and death.*[2]

If I have committed only one serious sin why should I go to Confession if my life is fundamentally faithful to Christ?

According to the *fundamental option theory,* in the event of committing one mortal sin a person does not lose the state of grace if the overall options he is making in life are fundamentally faithful to Christ's teachings. The Church, however, has identified this view as false and misleading.[3] It would be unfair to accuse the Church of downplaying God's mercy here because the reasons for which it considers this view as erroneous are sound as we shall see. By saying that the state of grace can be lost by one mortal sin the Church is not portraying God as a tyrant trying to catch us out. On the contrary, God is generous in the grace He gives to a person right up to his dying moments to help him die in the state of grace if he has not been presumptuous about God's mercy. Nor can the Church be accused of being too "act-oriented" (that is, being preoccupied with the sinful actions themselves rather than the persons involved. The teaching authority of the Church knows only too well that all of our sinful actions come from our free decisions, and that these choices emerge from the desires of our hearts. Our characters determine our ultimate destiny after death, yes, but our actions express and determine our characters.

The fallacy of the fundamental option theory can be further understood when we consider friendship. A person has to act in a hostile way towards his friend only once to break his friendship. Even if he has not fundamentally rejected his friend, his friendship will remain broken if he does not express sorrow for the harm he has caused. If this is true of human relationships,

---

[2] *Reconciliatio et Paenitentia,* no. 17.

[3] cf. Pope John Paul II, *Veritatis Splendor,* (1993), no. 65.

then why would it be any different with our relationship with Christ? How can we call ourselves Christ's friends if we deliberately choose to act contrary to His will in a serious matter and see no need to be reconciled with Him? This question is of greater importance when we understand that sin is not simply about breaking a *Commandment*, but about breaking our friendship with *Christ*.

Although the fundamental option theory is an attempt to portray the bountiful mercy of God, it can deceive us into becoming complacent or even presumptuous about His mercy. If a person was to take God's mercy for granted he would only be fooling himself. For this reason, God warns those who think that such a person's fate is unjust:

> *...is what I do unjust? Is it not what you do that is unjust? When the upright man renounces his integrity to commit sin and dies because of this, he dies because of the evil that he himself has committed.*[4]

Notice what the Lord is saying here. God is speaking about an "upright man," a man who has "integrity." According to the fundamental option theory, this must mean that the overall choices this man is making in his life are fundamentally faithful to the Commandments, and that therefore, by committing only one mortal sin he is still in the state of grace. However, this is not what the Scriptures tell us. Due to this man's sin he "dies [spiritually] because of this." Despite his overall integrity, "he dies because of the evil that he himself has committed."

Furthermore, if it can be argued that a single act cannot *deprive* someone of the state of grace, then it could also be argued that a single act could not be enough to *return* a person to grace or to *merit* grace. Such a contradiction illustrates how misleading the fundamental option theory is, especially when you consider that the single free choice the Good Thief made when he was on his cross on Good Friday was so meritorious that it enabled him to enter into Paradise immediately on his death, for Jesus said to him, "Truly, I say to you, *today* you will be with me in Paradise."[5] That one choice not only determined his eternal destiny; its effect was instantaneous. Conversely, when a person falls into mortal sin, that sin also has an effect that is immediate: "spiritual death," as

---

[4] Ezek 18:25-26. (*JB*)

[5] Lk 23:43.

Pope John Paul II described it.[6] Notice how the Church has not used any euphemisms here. Does a loving mother speak in euphemisms when her children are in serious danger? To this you may ask, "But is the Church really our *mother?*" St Cyprian of Carthage said that "no one can have God as Father who does not have the Church as mother."[7] And as our mother, it is reassuring to know that she guides us accordingly. In his own effort to provide such good guidance Pope John Paul II tried to dispel the widespread confusion that the fundamental option theory has brought about:

> *Care will have to be taken not to reduce mortal sin to an act of "fundamental option" – as is commonly said today – against God, intending thereby an explicit and formal contempt for God or neighbour. For mortal sin exists also when a person knowingly and willingly, for whatever reason, chooses something gravely disordered. In fact, such a choice already includes contempt for the divine law, a rejection of God's love for humanity and the whole of creation; the person turns away from God and loses charity. Thus the fundamental orientation can be radically changed by individual acts. Clearly there can occur situations which are very complex and obscure from a psychological viewpoint and which have an influence on the sinner's subjective culpability. But from a consideration of the psychological sphere one cannot proceed to the construction of a theological category, which is what the "fundamental option" precisely is, understanding it in such a way that it objectively changes or casts doubt upon the traditional concept of mortal sin.*[8]

---

[6] *Reconciliatio et Paenitentia,* no. 17.

[7] St Cyprian, *De unit.* 6: PL 4, 519, cited in *CCC,* no. 181.

[8] *Reconciliatio et Paenitentia,* no. 17.

Appendix D: True Stories – the Seal of Confession Unbroken Under Pressure

In chapter three we noted that since Christ is encountered in Confession through the ministry of the priest, it follows that your confession is only between you and God. The following two stories are about some priests who remained faithful to the Seal of Confession under immense pressure. Such stories not only help penitents to have a greater confidence in Confession, they also provide no shortage of inspiration to priests in their desire to represent Christ faithfully in this sacrament.

St John Nepomucene (1340-1393)

The Patron Saint of Confession, St John Nepomucene, was martyred for the Seal. He was a priest of Prague who was put under immense pressure by the King of Bohemia, Wenceslaus IV. He had asked St John to disclose what his beautiful queen, Sophie, had said in Confession. When he refused the king had him imprisoned. Despite torture and the king's death threats, he did not break the Seal. Consequently, the king ordered St John to be executed. On 20 March 1393 he was burned, tied to a wheel and thrown off a bridge into the Moldau River.

Father Dumoulin

The following true story was published in *The Freeman's Journal* (Cooperstown, New York, 23 April, 1892):

> *An interesting story, showing with what inviolable secrecy the revelations made in the confessional are guarded, has just come to light. Three years ago a Catholic priest, the Abbe Dumoulin, of the Archdiocese of Aix, France, was tried and convicted of murder to the utter consternation of the Catholic population, by whom he*

was much revered. The victim of the murder was a Madame Blanchard, a wealthy and pious lady, and the evidence, though entirely circumstantial, was sufficient to convict the accused priest.

Madame was president of a Catholic charitable association, and in that capacity she called one day at the parochial residence to remove some funds deposited with Fr Dumoulin: the amount of 12,000 Francs, which Fr Dumoulin gave her on demand … Mme Blanchard did not return to her home that evening, and her family became alarmed and searched for her unavailingly. Four days later her body was discovered in one of the empty cells of the old monastery. It bore marks of a violent death from stabs with a knife, and the money she had received was gone.

Search was then made in the presbytery and one of the table knives was found covered with human blood and also a handkerchief belonging to the dead woman, in which presumably the money had been rolled. Suspicion at once fell on Fr Dumoulin, who was, by his own statement, the last person who had seen Madame Blanchard alive. He was tried and convicted and sentenced to transportation for life – sentence of death not being inflicted, partly on account of his former unblemished character and partly through the nature of the evidence.

The occurrence excited much comment at the time but was gradually forgotten, and Fr Dumoulin was only remembered as an awful instance of human depravity by most of his former parishioners. Some five months ago, however, a startling revelation occurred. Kloser, the sexton, was stricken with remorse and publicly confessed that it was himself who had murdered Madame Blanchard for the sake of plunder. He detailed all the circumstances of his crime with minute precision. He knew that the lady had a large sum in her possession and procuring a knife from the kitchen he waylaid her in the corridor, stabbed her to death and threw the body into a cell where it was subsequently found. The knife stained with blood and the handkerchief he hid again in the presbytery and kept himself out of sight for some time.

The most remarkable fact was that the day after the body was discovered he was struck with remorse for his crime and told it in confession to Fr Dumoulin himself. The latter, when afterwards accused of the murder, made no attempt to exculpate himself, even by casting suspicion on the real culprit, who thus actually was protected by the priest's self-devotion. He not only guarded the secret of the confessional but lest he might impair its obligation he refrained from even suggesting that the sexton could have committed the murder - a suggestion which he would naturally have made had not the crime been fully revealed to him in the sacred tribunal. In view of Kloser's full confession the Superior Court at Aix formally decreed a new trial for Fr Dumoulin, when he was unanimously acquitted of the crime of which he had been so wrongly adjudged guilty. His return to his church after nearly three years' exile was the occasion of a demonstration of the most striking kind, and he is now again employed in the work of his ministry after giving the world one more lesson of what the seal of confession means for a Catholic priest.

Appendix E: Plenary Indulgence

In chapter nine we noted that an indulgence is a benefit that sincerely repentant Catholics can obtain that can diminish the temporal punishment due to their sins as soon as possible. In addition to the prescribed works described below, the following four conditions need to be observed for the reception of each indulgence:

(i) Receiving sacramental confession and absolution within 8 days before or after performing the prescribed work;

(ii) reception of Holy Communion;

(iii) prayer for the intentions of the Pope. This particular condition is fully satisfied by reciting one Our Father and one Hail Mary. Nevertheless, you are free to recite any other prayer according to your piety and devotion.

(iv) All attachment to sin, even venial sin, must be absent. If the latter disposition is in any way less than perfect or if the three conditions prescribed above are not fulfilled, the indulgence will be only partial.

Prescribed Works

The full list of the grants of plenary indulgences are contained in *Enchiridion Indulgentiarum (Handbook of Indulgences)* originally issued by the Apostolic Penitentiary in 1968 to implement Paul VI's *Indulgentiarum Doctrina.* The current fourth edition in Latin (July 1999) of the *Enchiridion* can be viewed on the following website:

For a list of the prescribed works in English see: *The Handbook of Indulgences - Norms and Grants* - Authorised English Edition (New York: Catholic Book Publishing Corp, 1991).

Appendix F: Guide for a Good Confession

When we go to Confession we need to (i) examine our conscience; (ii) have contrition; (iii) confess our sins; (iv) receive absolution; and (v) do penance. Below is a step-by-step procedure along with some practical guidance as to what these steps involve. It is divided into two main parts: *preparation for the Sacrament of Reconciliation* and the *procedure in the confessional.*

Preparation for the Sacrament of Reconciliation

Examination of Conscience

To help you examine your conscience the following lists of sins are based upon the *Ten Commandments* and the *Precepts of the Church.* Although these sins involve serious matter, they would not be mortal if you committed them without sufficient knowledge and deliberate consent. As for venial sins, although they can be forgiven without sacramental confession the Church nevertheless recommends we confess them because while they do not extinguish sanctifying grace they still incur temporal punishment and stunt our spiritual growth.[1]

The Ten Commandments

The Ten Commandments are the basic moral commands given by God to Moses (cf. Ex 20:1-17; Deut 5:6-21), renewed and amplified by Christ (cf. Mt 5:19, 21-22, 27-28).

First Commandment

"I am the Lord your God: you shall not have strange gods before me."

☐ Have I denied the existence of God? Have I deliberately refused to hold as true what God has revealed and the Church proposes for belief?

[1] cf. *CCC,* no. 1863.

- ☐ Have I deliberately taught anything heretical, that is, anything which dissents from the doctrines of our Faith?
- ☐ Have I been indifferent, ungrateful, or hateful towards God?
- ☐ Have I, through despair, deliberately refused to hope for or appeal to God's mercy?
- ☐ Have I been presumptuous about God's mercy by hoping to obtain His forgiveness without repentance?
- ☐ Have I been involved in *occult practices* such as séances, using a ouija board, or the worship of Satan?
- ☐ Have I engaged in *superstitious practices*? Have I consulted horoscopes, clairvoyants or other mediums such as palm readers and fortune tellers?

Second Commandment

"*You shall not take the Name of the Lord your God in vain.*"

- ☐ Have I committed *blasphemy* (contempt for God in thought, word, or action), or *profanity* (used the Lord's name in vain) with deliberate disrespect?
- ☐ Have I committed the sin of *sacrilege* (profaning a sacred person, place, or thing)?
- ☐ Have I committed *perjury* (telling a lie under oath)?
- ☐ Have I sought the approval of others in an attempt to be more socially acceptable to the point of scandalising or demeaning God's holy name or His Church?

Third Commandment

"*Remember to keep holy the Lord's Day.*"

- ☐ Have I neglected to worship God at Mass on Sundays and on holy days of obligation? (In Australia the holy days of obligation are *Christmas Day* and the *Assumption of Mary,* 15 August.)
- ☐ Have I failed to participate fully and actively in Mass on Sundays through my own fault by not being present during its three principal parts, namely, the *Presentation of the Gifts, Consecration* and the *priest's Communion*) thereby failing to fulfil the Sunday obligation?

Fourth Commandment

"Honour your father and your mother."

- ☐ Do I honour my parents and my extended family? Have I been disobedient and disrespectful towards them?
- ☐ Have I reacted proudly and hurt my parents when they correct me?
- ☐ Have I neglected the needs of my parents or extended family members in their old age or in time of need?
- ☐ Have I purposely refused to help someone in serious need when I had the opportunity and the means to do so?
- ☐ As a parent, have I neglected the religious education of my children?
- ☐ Have I done my duty by my country?

Fifth Commandment

"You shall not kill."

- ☐ When hurt by others, do I desire revenge, harbour anger, hatred, or resentment to the point of wishing them evil?
- ☐ Have I wished someone evil through hatred, or desired to deliberately hurt or kill someone through envy or anger?
- ☐ Have I committed *extortion?* That is, have I attempted to obtain something that impoverishes someone's livelihood in a major way by coercion or intimidation?
- ☐ Have I used *unnecessary aggression* in self-defence that has killed or seriously injured someone who has attacked me (that is, force that is disproportionate to the harm used against me)?
- ☐ Have I unjustly and intentionally killed a human being?
- ☐ Have I inflicted grievous bodily harm on another person or threatened someone with serious physical, verbal or emotional abuse?
- ☐ Have I swore at someone with deliberate disrespect?
- ☐ Have I mutilated myself? Did I get drunk or take narcotic drugs? Have I sold or given prohibited drugs to others? Have I eaten excessively to the point of gluttony?
- ☐ Have I deliberately driven a vehicle recklessly or under the influence of alcohol or drugs?
- ☐ Have I ever seriously considered or attempted *suicide* (to take my own life)?
- ☐ Have I promoted, encouraged, or supported the practice of *euthanasia* (assisted suicide or mercy killing)?

- ☐ Have I procured, cooperated in, or performed an abortion? Have I recommended or encouraged someone to have one?
- ☐ Have I used the "morning after pill" or some potentially abortion-causing drug?

Sixth Commandment

"You shall not commit adultery."

and

Ninth Commandment

"You shall not covet [desire unlawfully] your neighbour's wife."

- ☐ Have I committed adultery by being sexually unfaithful to my marriage, or if I am not married, have I been sexually active with a married person?
- ☐ Have I committed rape or incest? Have I engaged in homosexual acts or any other sexual activity outside of marriage?
- ☐ Have I committed fornication (pre-marital sex)?
- ☐ Have I committed impure acts against my own body or someone else's body?
- ☐ Have I given in to lust, entertained impure thoughts, or put myself into occasions of sin by viewing immoral movies, reading 'trashy' novels, or having recourse to pornographic material or websites?
- ☐ Have I used artificial means of birth control or have I had an operation to render myself sterile for contraceptive purposes?
- ☐ Have I participated in immoral methods of conceiving a child through in vitro fertilisation (IVF) or artificial insemination?
- ☐ Have I deliberately made uninvited and unwelcome sexual advances toward another or have I purposely dressed immodestly to seduce others?
- ☐ Have I engaged in impure conversations or told dirty jokes?
- ☐ Have I engaged in sexual foreplay with a deliberate desire to arouse passion reserved for marriage, thereby putting myself and the one I love in danger of more grievous sins?
- ☐ Am I living in an occasion of sin by *co-habiting* (living alone with my boyfriend or girlfriend), or sharing a room with a person I am attracted to?
- ☐ Do I have friendships which are habitual occasions of sin? If so, have I not made any effort to distance myself from these occasions?

Seventh Commandment

"You shall not steal."

and

Tenth Commandment

"You shall not covet [desire unlawfully] your neighbour's goods."

- ☐ Did I entertain/indulge a desire to steal?
- ☐ Have I taken someone else's property against the reasonable will of the owner?
- ☐ Have I wilfully damaged, defaced, destroyed, or lost someone's property and made no effort to make restitution?
- ☐ Did I cheat in an examination or in business?
- ☐ Have I neglected the essential needs of others by a serious disregard for the poor, tax evasion, defrauding labourers of their wages, laziness, making no effort to return lost goods to their owner, holding grudges, or greed?
- ☐ Have I effected the livelihood of others through cheating, gambling, wilful neglect of debts, racial prejudice or discrimination, sins against the environment, etc?

Eighth Commandment

"You shall not bear false witness against your neighbour."

- ☐ Have I lied? Am I honest in my dealings with others? Have I knowingly and wilfully deceived someone?
- ☐ Have I deliberately committed *calumny* or *slander* (telling derogatory lies about others, calling people names, or spreading rumours about them), *detraction* (telling the faults of others without necessity), or *libel* (writing lies about others) so as to destroy their reputation? Have I deliberately neglected to repair the damage caused by these sins?
- ☐ Have I accused someone else unjustly to get myself out of trouble?
- ☐ Did I deliberately betray someone's confidence in me without due cause or through gossip?
- ☐ Have I deliberately told a lie in an attempt to be exalted?

The Precepts of the Church

It is a serious matter for a Catholic to fail to observe any of the Precepts of the Church[2] without grave reason because they were established to help us avoid violating some of the Ten Commandments that are often breached (examples of grave reason would be having no reasonable means to get to a church, the demands of charity, or ill health.)

First Precept

"You shall attend Mass on Sundays and on holy days of obligation."

- ☐ See the Third Commandment, "*Remember to keep holy the Lord's Day.*"

Second Precept

"You shall confess your serious sins at least once a year."

- ☐ Have I put off going to Confession for over a year when I was in mortal sin?
- ☐ Did I deliberately conceal any serious sins in my previous Confession(s)? Do I realise that this makes this sacrament *sacrilegious* and *invalid* and that in a subsequent Confession I must confess that I have knowingly withheld serious sins?

Third Precept

"You shall humbly receive your Creator in Holy Communion at least during the Easter season."

- ☐ Have I not received Holy Communion during Mass for over a year without grave reason?
- ☐ Have I received Holy Communion in a state of un-confessed mortal sins without grave reason?

Fourth Precept

"You shall observe the prescribed days of fasting and abstinence."

- ☐ Have I abstained from meat and fasted when we are obliged to do so (Ash Wednesday and Good Friday)?
- ☐ Have I exercised some form of penance or work of charity appropriate to my life on the Fridays of Lent, and the Fridays throughout the year?[3]

Fifth Precept

"You shall observe the laws of the Church regarding marriage."

- ☐ Did I marry in a Catholic church? If not, did I obtain permission from the Church?
- ☐ Have I divorced and remarried without an annulment?

Sixth Precept

"The faithful also have the duty of providing for the material needs of the Church, according to their abilities."

- ☐ Do I contribute to the needs of the Church and its pastors by offering a just and reasonable amount of my time, talents and/or money appropriate to my way of life?

Contrition

Without *contrition* we cannot receive God's forgiveness. "Contrition" comes from the Latin word, "*contritio,*" meaning a "*wearing down*" of that which is hardened. It is the disposition with which we try to overcome hardness of heart by sorrow and detestation for our sins and the resolution not to sin again. This means that we have a *firm purpose of amendment.* The *purpose* of amendment is not the *certitude* of amendment but a sincere resolve, with the help of God's grace, not to sin again. This resolution necessarily means being willing to avoid the *occasions of sin* (persons, places, things, or any act that previously led us into sin or made us susceptible to sin). As we can see, the sorrow for our sins that we need to have to receive this sacrament is more than just being aware that we have done something morally wrong.

---

[2] cf. *CIC,* cans. 1246-1248, 989, 920, 1246, 1249-1251, 1108, 222 respectively.

[3] The Australian Bishops Conference has not restricted our penance to fast and abstinence in all cases on the Fridays throughout the year for it has left room for our own responsible choice in accordance with *CIC,* can. 1253. If we choose an alternative to fasting and abstinence, in whole or in part for other forms of penance, such as works of charity or exercises of piety, we should carefully select the form of penance that we consider most appropriate for our own circumstances and growth in the Christian life.

Procedure in the Confessional

Greeting

After the priest welcomes you, make the sign of the Cross, saying: *"Bless me Father for I have sinned. It has been (say how long) since my last confession."* The priest may give you a blessing and/or read a short passage of Scripture.

Confession of Sins

You now have the opportunity to tell God all the things you wish to confess. Ask God to give you the courage to make a good confession. If you are conscious of any serious sins you need to confess them in kind and number as far as you can recall. You do not need to provide explicit details, unless you think the circumstances influence the nature of the sin. If you are anxious or afraid be sure to tell the priest as he will help you. At this stage you also have the opportunity to ask the priest questions regarding any matter you are unsure about. When you have made your confession, finish with: *"For these and all my past sins I am truly sorry."* The priest may give some words of encouragement and advice.

Penance

The Priest will now give you some penance to do. If you are unable to perform the penance he proposes you may ask for another. This penance is not performed now but within a reasonable time after you depart from the confessional.

Act of Contrition

You are now invited to express your sorrow, which you may do in these or similar words:

> My God,
> I am sorry for my sins with all my heart.
> In choosing to do wrong
> and failing to do good,
> I have sinned against you

whom I should love above all things.
I firmly intend, with your help,
to do penance, to sin no more,
and to avoid whatever leads me to sin.
Our Saviour Jesus Christ suffered and died for us.
In his name, my God, have mercy. Amen.

or:

O my God,
I am sorry that I have sinned against you.
Because you are so good,
and with your help,
I will not sin again. Amen.

Absolution

This is the moment when Christ forgives you through the ministry of the Church and the words of absolution. While he extends his hands, or at least his right hand over your head, he blesses you with the sign of the Cross and says: *"... I absolve you from your sins in the name of the Father, and of the Son, and of the Holy Spirit."* In faith we believe that Christ says these words through the ministry of the priest. To this you answer: "Amen."

Dismissal

The priest will dismiss you using these or similar words: *"The Lord has freed you from your sins. Go in peace."* After which you say: *"Thanks be to God."* It is a pious practice to pray for the priest who has absolved you while making thanksgiving after Confession.

Abbreviations

The following are abbreviations cited in the footnotes:

CCC	*Catechism of the Catholic Church*
cf	cited from
CIC	*Codex Iuris Canonici* (*Code of Canon Law,* 1983)
DS	Denzinger-Schönmetzer, *Enchiridion Symbolorum, definitionum et declarationum de rebus fidei et morum* (1965)

The following abbreviations are used for the books of the Bible cited in the text:

Gen	Genesis	Lk	Luke
Ex	Exodus	Jn	John
Lev	Leviticus	Acts	Acts of the Apostles
Deut	Deuteronomy	Rom	Romans
Judg	Judges	1 Cor	1 Corinthians
2 Chr	2 Chronicles	2 Cor	2 Corinthians
Esth	Esther	Gal	Galations
Job	Job	Eph	Ephesians
Ps	Psalm	Phil	Philippians
Prov	Proverbs	Col	Colossians
Wis	Wisdom	2 Thess	2 Thessalonians
Sir	Sirach	1 Tim	1 Timothy
Isa	Isaiah	2 Tim	2 Timothy
Jer	Jeremiah	Heb	Hebrews
Ezek	Ezekial	Jas	James
Dan	Daniel	1 Pet	1 Peter
Joel	Joel	2 Pet	2 Peter
Mt	Matthew	1 Jn	1 John
Mk	Mark	Rev	Revelation

Index

Index of Scripture Citations
Old Testament

New Testament

2 Corinthians

Galatians

Ephesians

Philippians

Colossians

2 Thessalonians

1 Timothy

2 Timothy

Hebrews

James

1 Peter

2 Peter

1 John

Revelation

www.ingramcontent.com/pod-product-compliance
Ingram Content Group UK Ltd.
Pitfield, Milton Keynes, MK11 3LW, UK
UKHW021055200726
13857UKWH00003B/927